THE UNOFFICIAL QUIZ BOOK

Think You Know

TV SOAPS?

Clive Gifford

a division of Hodder Headline Limited

© Hodder Children's Books 2004

Published in Great Britain in 2004
by Hodder Children's Books

Editor: Hayley Leach
Design by Fiona Webb
Cover design: Hodder Children's Books

The right of Clive Gifford to be identified as the author
of the work has been asserted by him in accordance with
the Copyright, Designs and Patents Act 1988.

10 9 8 7 6 5 4 3 2 1

ISBN: 0340878703

Printed by Bookmarque Ltd, Croydon, Surrey

The paper and board used in this paperback by Hodder
Children's Books are natural recyclable products made
from wood grown in sustainable forests. The manufacturing
processes conform to the environmental regulations of the
country of origin.

Hodder Children's Books
a division of Hodder Headline Limited
338 Euston Road
London NW1 3BH

Contents

Introduction

So you think you know all about the Soaps? Think you can untangle the complex alliances and betrayals, trace the complicated family ties and know your Soap heroes from villains? Well you will need all your wits and knowledge to recall the loves and lies, the babies and betrayals, the weddings and workplaces, the affairs and addictions. Some of the questions are more difficult than the most tearaway foster child in *Home and Away*. Others are even more dastardly than *Coronation Street's* serial killer and *EastEnders'* Mitchell Brothers and Dirty Den combined.

This book contains 1,050 questions on six of the most popular TV Soaps: *EastEnders, Coronation Street, Hollyoaks, Emmerdale, Home and Away* and *Neighbours*. Each of the soaps is represented by a symbol (see below). The questions are organised into easy , medium   and hard quizzes with 50 questions per quiz. All the answers are found at the back of the book but cheating will see you barred from Lou's Place, the Rovers Return, the Woolpack and the Queen Vic at the very least.

Good luck!

Clive Gifford

Symbols for each soap:

Neighbours

Coronation Street

EastEnders

Emmerdale

Home and Away

Hollyoaks

EASY Questions

1. Which *Emmerdale* family has had the most members in the show: the Armstrongs, the Sugdens or the Dingles?

2. *EastEnders* is set in Watford, Walford, Walthamstow or Woking?

3. What is the name of the pub in Erinsborough?

4. Which family includes Kat, Zoe and Charlie?

5. Jarvis Skelton and Edna Birch entered into a war of words over: wheelie bins, grazing rights for cows or cheating at dominoes?

6. Ken Barlow and Tracy Barlow were held in a siege in a supermarket: true or false?

7. Who worked as a lifeguard before being paralysed in a car accident?

8. Jimmy Kelly left Jack Duckworth a valuable vase, a garden allotment or his old record collection?

9. Which *Pop Idol* star made a guest appearance in *Hollyoaks* during July 2003?

10. Who wrote a marriage proposal to Sally on her class blackboard: Alf, Donald or Flynn?

11. Which senior figure in *Hollyoaks* has a daughter called Mandy and owns Washed Up?

12. Who tried to kill his family by driving their car into the canal?

13. *Coronation Street* is set in Manchester, Newcastle, Leeds or Liverpool?

14. Who was the estate manager of Home Farm before a bust up with Chris Tate: Seth Armstrong, Marlon Dingle or Jack Sugden?

15. Which family ran the caravan park until Josh West took over?

16. Chauffeur Biff Fowler had an affair with Lady Tara: true or false?

17. Who is Vicki Fowler's grandmother: Pat, Pauline or Dot?

18. Which *Neighbours* character suffered with amnesia and didn't recognise her husband at all?

19. Who is Morag's brother: Noah, Rhys or Alf?

20. Warrinor is a neighbouring district of Erinsborough: true or false?

21. Flynn was the owner of the drugs found during woodwork class at Summer Bay High: true or false?

22. Who was married to Barry but had an affair with Ricky?

23. Who split up with Angie to declare his feelings for Leah: Noah, Jesse or Flynn?

24. Is Peggy: Phil, Barry or Jamie's mother?

25. Who is the eldest son of the Marsden family: Ali, Paul or Roderick?

26. Which female resident of Summer Bay is a major gossip and owns a mobile home in the caravan park?

27. Who hit Charity in 2003 during a row over their daughter?

28. Karen McDonald is married to Steve, Jim or Lee?

29. Dale Jackson is a policeman, a policewoman, a VAT inspector or a traffic warden?

30. What is the surname of the long running Corrie characters Jack and Vera?

31. Who organised a poker night at the Loft: Scott, Dan, Toby or Tony?

32. What is the name of the pub in *Coronation Street*?

33. Name one of the two families who have traditionally run the fruit and veg stall in Walford market.

34. *Neighbours* centres on the lives of the inhabitants of which Australian street?

35. Is Beth: Scott, Nick, Hayley or Seb's mum?

36. In which city is *EastEnders* set?

37. Which *EastEnders* lady was a Butcher before she was an Evans?

38. Who turned out to be *Hollyoaks'* 2003 serial killer?

39. Who was the longest serving cleaner of the Rovers Return: Harry Flagg, Hilda Ogden or Vera Duckworth?

40. What is the canine name of the pub in *Hollyoaks*?

41. A film set arrived in *Emmerdale* in April 2003. Was it for a Hollywood blockbuster, a Japanese documentary or a Bollywood film?

42. Which *Neighbours* cast member has a very seasonal first name?

43. Alfie Moon was in prison before he became pub manager at the Vic: true or false?

44. Where did Dawn and Terry meet: in Spain, in the Woolpack, at the holiday village or in London?

45. Which older Summer Bay resident had a brain tumour: Irene, Alf or Morag?

46. At what complex, beginning with the letter L, is the local doctor's surgery found?

47. What was the name of Pauline Fowler's husband?

48. Who donates a kidney to his old rival, Lou Carpenter?

49. Max organised an illegal raffle to try to buy the caravan park: true or false?

50. Who decides to accompany Chloe on a year-long trip to Australia?

QUIZ 2

1. Around which bay is *Home and Away* set?

2. Which famous pop star played Beth Brennan in *Neighbours*?

3. What is the name of the long-serving pub in *EastEnders*?

4. Is *Emmerdale* set in Lancashire, Yorkshire or Devon?

5. Inside what stuffed Australian animal was a mysterious white powder found by Lou and Connor?

6. Did the powder turn out to be: rat poison, a cure for baldness, flour or baking soda?

7. Which Corrie businessman has had four wives?

8. In 2003, who embarked on a secret affair with Helen Cunningham?

9. Is Cain's surname: Dingle, Woods or Hope?

10. Martin Fowler is the secret son of Kat Slater: true or false?

11. Which Summer Bay youngster was a graffiti artist?

12. What is the name of the area in which *Neighbours* is set?

13. Is Terence a female or male dog?

14. Seth Armstrong was a poacher, a TV presenter or a farm owner before he became a gamekeeper?

15. What is the name of Mike Baldwin's clothing business?

16. In *Hollyoaks*, what does HCC stand for?

17. What sort of shop does Lucy Richards run: a florists, a bakers or a gift card store?

18. What plant does Tomiko give Sam as a farewell present: a geranium, a bonsai tree or a date palm?

19. Pauline Fowler was married to Arthur for 13, 23, 31 or 51 years before he died?

20. What was the name of Harold Bishop's wife who died in 2001?

21. What was the name of the fast food venue with which the Bayside Diner had to compete: Brilliant Burgers, Tasty Feed, Bonza Burger or Frying Tonight?

22. In which fictional part of the East End is *EastEnders* set?

23. What colour is the hat which is frequently seen on Edna Birch's head: blue, red or green?

24. The Weatherfield Arms is a rival pub to the Rovers Return: true or false?

25. Who is the owner of Dan's Pit Stop?

26. What is the name of the school featured in *Home and Away*?

27. Which doctor renewed his wedding vows with his wife in 2003?

28. Robbie Jackson has a sister – can you name her?

29. Where was Marlon and Tricia's wedding reception held: in Hope Farm, Chez Marlon Restaurant or the Woolpack?

30. Which mother and daughter have both had a relationship with Dev Alahan?

31. Zara failed her first driving test: true or false?

32. What was Curly Watts' real first name?

33. Who became Dan Hunter's first regular girlfriend in *Hollyoaks*: Mandy Richardson, Debbie Dean or Chloe Bruce?

34. Who became acting principal of Summer Bay High when Donald Fisher temporarily retired?

35. Who took in the stray dog, Tootsie, after her own dog, Batley, died?

36. Dr Karl Kennedy is Ben Kirk's grandfather: true or false?

37. Who is the youngest member of the Nelson household: Angela, Craig or Katy?

38. Mandy Richardson has dated two *Hollyoaks* men who have since died in the show: true or false?

39. Redhead teenager Fiona Brown is better known by what nickname?

40. Is Alex and Leah's Dad called: Dimitri Theo, Leonard or Costas?

41. Who is forced to pay for an expensive new pair of trainers after burying a stinking old pair?

42. Who confronted her father, who had abused her, in the 1000th episode of *Hollyoaks*?

43. At whose hairdressing salon did Sarah spend a week on work experience?

44. What does Shadrach spend his money for trainers on instead: a new shirt, a pub lunch or a country and western CD?

45. What nationality is Jack Osborne: Australian, Scottish, Welsh or English?

46. Which *Coronation Street* character was once married to Samir Rachid?

47. Did Alex sell his car, his guitar collection or his share of a business to come up with the money to give to Leah?

48. Who tells Ruby Dwyer that she has an addiction to gambling: Dee, Rosie, Steph or Susan?

49. What is the name of Will Smith's wife: Geena, Gypsy or Jennifer?

50. Which country does VJ have to go to for an operation?

1. *Neighbours* character, Jarrod Rebecchi, is better known by what nickname?

2. What sort of special dancing event occurred in the Woolpack in March 2003: ballroom dancing, nude dancing, line dancing or disco dancing?

3. Eileen Grimshaw has two sons. Can you name either of them?

4. Near which city is *Hollyoaks* set?

5. Which young child does Clare act as a nanny for: Sarah, Bethany or Joshua?

6. Kirk Sutherland won a huge amount of wool, bags of compost or toilet paper in a competition?

7. Who tells everyone in the Woolpack pub about Ronnie Marsden's affair with Louise: Jack Sugden, Paul Marsden or Andy Sugden?

8. Which girl was involved in the robbing of the Minute Mart?

9. Which resident of Ramsay Street considers himself a fine tuba player?

10. What is the name of Kirsty's twin sister?

11. What is the name of Natalie and Barry's son?

12. Who did Terry Woods marry in 2003?

13. Which burger vendor's best mate is OB?

14. Which young Summer Bay girl had a tough fight against alcohol addiction in 2003?

15. How much money did Robbie gain from his real father: £100, £1,000, £10,000 or £100,000?

16. Who is an ambulance called for after a drinking game by the cricket pavilion goes wrong: Donna, Viv, Lisa or Charity?

17. The Loft club was closed down for gambling: true or false?

18. Which male resident of *Coronation Street* is Weatherfield's biggest gossip: Norris Cole, Steve McDonald or Jack Duckworth?

19. Viv was upset with Donna, Sam, Dawn or Syd getting a lip ring piercing?

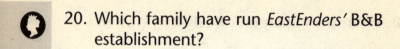

20. Which family have run *EastEnders'* B&B establishment?

21. What was Dee Bliss's real first name: Darcy, Diana, Dione or Deirdre?

22. Kylie or Danni Minogue made their name in *Home and Away* before starting an singing career?

23. What is the name of the doctor who arrived in the square in 2000 and has since been involved with several Slater sisters?

24. Who is in charge of the doctor's surgery in *Neighbours*?

25. What is the first name of Edna Birch's son: Peter, Paul or Jacob?

26. Which character had a one-night-stand with Tracy Barlow and confessed all to his wife shortly afterwards?

27. Where is Hollyoaks FM broadcast from?

28. Roy Cropper is the proprietor of which *Coronation Street* eating place?

29. What is the name of the pub in *Emmerdale*?

30. Candace Barkham is Harold Bishop's ex-wife: true or false?

31. Who turned out to have killed Angie Russell but says it was in self-defence?

32. Stuart Parker is also known by what nickname: Toadfish, Chooka or Drongo?

33. Which *EastEnders* car dealer lost his father and found out his wife was cheating on him in 2003?

34. Jerry McKinley works as a farmer, a landlord or a builder?

35. What is the two lettered abbreviation used for the son of Leah and Vinnie?

36. Who was *Coronation Street's* resident policewoman: Gail Hillman, Emma Watts or Tracy Barlow?

37. Ellie came up with pole dancing, fancy dress, karaoke or live bands as a way of improving business at the Loft?

38. What was the first name of Edna's granddaughter: Eve, Jennifer or Kylie?

39. Who tried to poison Mandy Richardson: Beth, Laura or Tony?

40. Which young *Neighbours* boy is caught, along with Daniel, spying on the Scully's bathroom?

41. Scott Hunter tried to kill Alf by setting light to the Beachside Diner: true or false?

42. Asif Malik had a crush on Janine Butcher: true or false?

43. What is the fictional area of the north-west in which *Coronation Street* is set?

44. How much did the winner of *Hollyoaks'* reality TV show receive: £100, £500, £1,000, £5,000 or £15,000?

45. Who did Lucy Richards marry in 2003?

46. Did Matt, OB or Nick buy Chloe a fish tank as a present?

47. What type of clothing does Mike Baldwin's factory make?

48. Who kissed Libby in September 2003 after having a crush on her for some time?

49. What is the name of the former wife of Dan Ferreira: Shirley, Pushpa or Gita?

50. Which double-glazing salesman is the brother of Bob Hope?

MEDIUM Questions

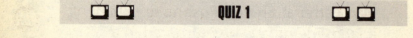

1. Which law graduate has also had a radio show on UNI FM?

2. Which member of the Marsden family kissed Louise Blackstock straight after the charity football match?

3. Who blindfolded Marlon prior to his wedding to Tricia: Bob Hope, Paddy Kirk or Seth Armstrong?

4. What is the name of Phil and Kathy's son: Ben, Ian or Martin?

5. Which jailbird returned to Summer Bay after spending eighteen months in prison?

6. Who was declared the winner of The Fish Tank competition?

7. Who moved into an empty canal barge only to find the lady he had had an affair with wanting to join him?

8. The Kennedy's eldest child lives in London with his wife. Is his name: Paul, Mal, Stephen or Kyle?

9. Ben Kirk's father died in a riding accident, a landslide or was he murdered in a robbery?

10. Which Asian businessman split with Tracy Barlow and has turned his attentions to one of his employees?

11. Who is devastated to learn that her boyfriend is the father of Zoe Tate's child?

12. Rachel Tate died when she was deliberately pushed off a cliff, pushed under a tractor or thrown into a sewage pond?

13. Which lady, along with Danny Hargreaves, opened D&S Hardware and DIY store?

14. In December of which year did *Neighbours* celebrate its 4,000th episode?

15. Who is Abby Davies' brother?

16. Who prepared a slushy birthday video for Natalie complete with him singing?

17. Annie Walker was an ex-landlady of the Rovers Return: true or false?

18. Jackson's Chippie is *Coronation Street's* local fish 'n' chip shop: true or false?

19. What is the name of Lance Smart's wife: Debbie, Laura or Geena?

20. Who did Spencer try to impress on New Year's Eve 2002?

21. Pop star Robbie Williams appeared as a background character in the Queen Vic in *EastEnders*: true or false?

22. Who is Little Mo's second husband?

23. Who did Shelley Unwin go to Mexico with: Steve McDonald, Peter Barlow or Tommy Nelson?

24. Which older *Neighbours* character used to play in a band called The Right Prescription?

25. Who became Izzy's deputy organiser of the water polo team?

26. Which Summer Bay resident has a son called Lance: Pippa, Colleen or Leah?

27. What newspaper settled with Libby Kennedy after refusing her a job they had previously offered?

28. Where did the South London Swordsmen plan to perform their saucy stripping act?

29. Did Roy Evans die from: a heart attack, a car accident, electrocution or an armed attack?

30. Who was killed during a mudslide: Bobby, Gavin, Saul or Shane?

31. Who takes Gino Esposito in as a lodger in his house?

32. Which *Emmerdale* character has a home-brewing system in his shed: Jarvis, Seth, Andy or Rodney?

33. What is the name of Kirk Sutherland's sister?

34. Who had an accident in a swimming pool and is told she may never walk again?

35. Diane Blackstock has a granddaughter called Gabrielle: true or false?

36. Laura Burns attacked and tried to kill which other *Hollyoaks* female?

37. What is the name of the spin-off to the Posh Gnosh restaurant in *Hollyoaks*?

38. Who is the eldest of Rhys Sutherland's children?

39. Who breaks in a door with her suitcase to discover that Roy Cropper has taken pills in a suicide attempt?

40. Which former partner of Little Mo's did Sam Mitchell have an affair with?

41. Whose partner becomes an MP and works a lot in Westminster, London?

42. Who sacks Les Battersby from Streetcars after he is charged with assaulting a police officer?

43. Alf and Ailsa Stewart's house was destroyed in 2000 by an earthquake, a gang fight, a mudslide or a gas explosion?

44. Who arrived in *EastEnders* after being kicked off a London Underground train: Alfie Moon, Dennis Rickman or Janine Butcher?

45. Who went shopping with Sunita and Deirdre for a wedding dress while her fiancé was booking a wedding with a different bride?

46. *Monty Python* star, Michael Palin, appeared as a surfer in the show: true or false?

47. Who punched Matti outside the church during Terry and Dawn's wedding?

48. What is the name of the father of Zoe's baby born in 2003?

49. Which *Hollyoaks* character is a keen rally driver, studied mechanics at college and opened his own auto store in the village?

50. Who shot an Afro-wearing commercial for his business in September 2003?

1. Which one of the following jobs has Stuart Parker not worked as: a hospital porter, a male stripper, a mechanic?

2. Which *Hollyoaks* character lost his brother in a potholing accident and has spent periods being homeless?

3. Who was killed when a fire broke out in the prison they were jailed in: Vinnie, Alf or Shane?

4. Who did Sunita Parekh fancy for a long time before he actually asked her out?

5. Boyd and Summer's mother was called Clare, Jackie, Helen or Maxine?

6. Who is made temporary manager of the Woolpack when Diane and Louise go on a holiday in May 2003?

7. Les struck up a bet with Mr C over who would get their learner driver to pass a driving test first, but who was Les teaching: Lee, Zara, Jodie or Bombhead?

8. And who was Mr C teaching to drive when he struck the bet?

9. Which member of the Scully family has a major fear of flying?

10. Who was engaged to Matt after having a one-night-stand with Alex?

11. Which character nearly married one of the Slater sisters before going out with Kat Slater?

12. Toadfish fell in love with which married woman: Susan Kennedy, Maggie Hancock or Lyn Scully?

13. Colleen Smart admits to having what sort of addiction in 2003?

14. Who asks Dot to marry him on a trip on the London Eye?

15. Saskia Duncan was murdered in which building in *EastEnders*?

16. Ashley Peacock works as: a barman, a butcher, a baker or a truck driver?

17. Did Charity, Angie or Zoe work in the past as a prostitute?

18. What is the name of Leah's brother?

 19. Which character is the only one to remain from the very first episodes of *Coronation Street*?

 20. What subject did Toadfish study at university?

 21. Who is the Smith children's foster mother?

 22. What item buried in the woods did Steph and the others try to retrieve in case it was found by the police?

 23. In which year did Karl and Susan have their 25th wedding anniversary: 1999, 2000, 2001 or 2002?

 24. Who set up his own building business in 2003 and got a job working on the Reynolds' house?

 25. Which member of the Reynolds family had a crush on Lady Tara?

 26. Who was Boyd Hoyland's first girlfriend?

27. Which married lady moved in with PC Mick Hopwood?

28. After being attacked on New Year's Eve 2002, did Izzy flee to the Davies' house, Gnosh Village, the Loft or the Cunningham's house?

29. Which lady works as the head chef at the diner in Summer Bay?

30. Who is Frankie Dean married to?

31. Ray Mullan came from Scotland, Wales, Ireland or Australia?

32. Nick Smith is accused of attacking which member of the Summer Bay High staff?

33. Who were married in a civil ceremony in Roy's Rolls Café in 1999?

34. Who bunks off school to go with her real father on several poaching trips?

35. Who is Lou's business partner in Lou's Place?

36. What is the name of Roy Cropper's wife?

37. What is the name of the female vet in *Emmerdale*?

38. Garry Hobbs is the father of Laura Dunn's child: true or false?

39. Who ditched Martin Fowler as he was about to attend court for the death of Jamie Mitchell?

40. Who pretends to be Spencer Moon to take a beating from Jack Dalton's thugs?

41. Who obtained a flock of chickens in Spring 2003 to conduct experiments on?

42. Which Sutherland girl finds herself attracted to both Seb Miller and Dylan?

43. Joe Carter ran a scam in 2003 to damage which other Corrie character's business?

44. Who showed a surprising temper in overturning a dinner table and smashing crockery in January 2003: Jack Duckworth, Ken Barlow, Curly Watts or Kirk Sutherland?

45. Which *Emmerdale* character has a sister called Latisha and a mother called Cynthia?

46. Which friend of Zoe Slater once worked as a prostitute and has lived in the Slater household?

47. Who was married to Bianca and had a child, Liam?

48. Who brought a horse to a party at the Dean's house?

49. What is the name of Ricky's date the night that the Minute Mart is burgled by Martin and Vicki?

50. Which *Emmerdale* character received a surprising £20,000 cheque from Chris Tate in August 2003?

 QUIZ 3

1. Did Chris, Charity or Debbie Tate ask for the charges against Cain Dingle to be dropped?

2. Which member of the Scully family works as a saleswoman for car spare parts?

29

3. Which girlfriend of Phil Mitchell turns out to be a policewoman?

4. Karen was about to forge Mike Baldwin's signature on a cheque when Mike walked in and signed the cheque himself. What sum was the cheque for: £2,500, £5,000, £10,000 or £25,000?

5. Harry Slater owned a bar in Minorca and dated Peggy: true or false?

6. With whom does Marlon have to share a room when he returns to Lisa's?

7. Who struggles to revise for her exams when Andy and Katie stay at her home?

8. Which country, a long way away from Walford, did Robbie Jackson visit in 2003?

9. Who spent Christmas 2002 in Greece without his wife as part of the Weatherfield Historical Society?

10. Who called the police to raid the Loft during a poker game causing the club to be closed down?

11. Who married Vinnie Patterson?

12. Which *Coronation Street* character is a male nurse?

13. What is the name of the tenant farmer who Chris Tate served with an eviction notice in early 2003?

14. Toadfish has a relative known as Stonefish: true or false?

15. Rhys Sutherland was an ex-professional player of which sport?

16. Daniel's bruises on his face are a result of a fight with Boyd, a fight with Summer or Daniel's Dad hitting him?

17. Who did Todd Grimshaw split up with in June 2003?

18. Who called in the police to arrest Cain Dingle for striking Charity?

19. Who was moving boxes which Alf Stewart was supposed to, only to die of a heart attack?

20. Which member of the Grimshaw family took a job as a Santa's Elf for Christmas 2002?

21. Ray Mullan is the son of Viv Windsor: true or false?

22. Which *Hollyoaks* character organised a water polo team?

23. Who put their back out when entering a New Year's Eve 2002 dancing competition?

24. Spencer got into hot water in May 2003 for passing fake £50 notes after he had sold: watches, out-of-date baked beans, used cars or computer parts?

25. Who barred Dennis Rickman from the Vic after seeing him upset Kat?

26. What is the name of Rhys Sutherland's nephew who has lived with his family?

27. Jacinta Martin bullied which *Neighbours* youngster who was performing her paper round?

28. Who is Mandy Richardson's step father?

29. What item of clothing did Izzy lose on New Year's Eve 2002 only for it to be found on the body of a murdered girl?

30. Which *Emmerdale* character has had three wives with the first names: Kathy, Rachel and Charity?

31. Who does Nita leave in charge of the Minute Mart before she goes travelling with Robbie?

32. Which teacher's classes did the students of Summer Bay High boycott in February 2003?

33. Blanche Hunt is which Corrie girl's grandmother?

34. Who was Lou Carpenter's wife until she died in a car crash: Cheryl, Rosie or Susan?

35. Which lady is to have Sally and Flynn's baby: Sophie, Colleen or Kirsty?

36. Who is promoted from an extra to the starring role of a bride in the Bollywood movie being filmed in *Emmerdale*?

37. Who is the father of Ben Kirk?

 38. Which previous cast member was a cousin of Toadfish and got memorably stung by a scorpion?

 39. Lewis quit the local *Hollyoaks* band when he discovered, Mandy Richardson, Helen Cunningham or Lucy Benson hid drugs in his guitar?

 40. Which member of the Sugden family hounded Stephen Butler because he thought he was a homosexual?

 41. What is the name of Sarah Platt's daughter?

 42. Who offers to fix the Loft's security webcam in order to start a money-making scam?

 43. Who won the football raffled after Maxine Peacock's death: Kirk Sutherland, Tommy Nelson or Aidan Critchley?

 44. Boyd is the best dancer in the Hoyland family: true or false?

45. What is the name of the gangland boss who entered the square in May 2003?

46. Colleen Smart had a crush on which ex-Summer Bay teacher?

47. Who was the first guest on Chloe's new 2003 radio show appearing to talk about his binge drinking and how he planned to give it up?

48. Who was Roy Evans about to hit when he had a heart attack?

49. What was the name of Taj Coppin's sister who was infamous as a bully and blackmailer?

50. Which older couple enjoy some drug-filled brownies given to them by Maz?

QUIZ 4

1. Which *Coronation Street* character repeatedly hit Emily Bishop with a crowbar: Les Battersby, Richard Hillman, Alan Bradley or Des Barnes?

2. By what name is Toadfish's Dad known: Big Mike, Big Kev, Big Pete or Big Al?

3. Linda, Mrs C or Frankie Dean is the mother of the *Hollyoaks* serial killer?

4. What was the name of the lady Karl Kennedy had an affair with?

5. Which *Hollyoaks* character was a fireman before becoming unemployed?

6. Who stepped in to find Emily Bishop being beaten, only to be killed herself?

7. Who was used as a 'body double' for photos over the internet to impress Roxy: Ben, Kristian, Jake Dean or Scott Anderson?

8. Harry Slater, Charlie Slater or Trevor Morgan turned out to be Zoe Slater's real father?

9. Who organised a scam involving live webcam pictures of pole dancing auditions: Tony Hutchinson, Craig Dean, Ben Davies or Mandy Richardson?

10. Jack Scully played football in England, but for which club: Arsenal, Barnsford, QPR or Cheltenham Rovers?

11. Which Ramsay Street house is nearest to the local school: number 32, number 28, number 24 or number 26?

12. Steph Stokes was the estranged mother of which *Emmerdale* character?

13. What does Susan Kennedy do for a living: work in a bar, run the coffee shop, work as a teacher or run a caravan park?

14. What natural disaster causes most of *Hollyoaks* to learn of Tony's affair with Helen Cunningham?

15. Who moved Angie Russell's body after she had been killed: Jade and Kirsty, Dani, Rhys or Irene Roberts?

16. Who is reported in the *Emmerdale* local newspaper as taking a mysterious lady to the ballet: Jack Sugden, Eric Pollard or Chris Tate?

17. Who was Roy Evans married to: Pat, Dot, Pauline or Kate?

18. Did Ailsa Stewart die of a gunshot wound, being suffocated by a mudslide, a heart attack or being hit by a runaway truck?

19. Who caught the rat which was released into The Fish Tank: Scott, Ellie or Chloe?

20. Who ran down and killed Sonia's boyfriend, Jamie?

21. Which of the following streets are featured in *Coronation Street*: Crimea Street, Jackson Street, Edward Street or Victoria Street?

22. A letter from which character persuades Sonia to attend Jamie's funeral?

23. Who employed a divorce lawyer for Laura to spite Ian Beale?

24. Spencer sold his consignment of baked bean tins for £120 to a farmer for pig swill: true or false?

25. Who is quizzed by a local DJ about missing council money: Mr C, Mrs C, Tony Hutchinson or Scott Anderson?

26. What is the name of the nanny Phil Mitchell first employed in September 2002?

27. Who discovered the body of Edna Miller lying in his own bed?

28. Who came out in a terrible rash after taking a herbal sleeping remedy suggested by Laurel Potts?

29. Who was struggling with his affections for Lori and Nina in May 2003?

30. Which member of the Scully family was left at the wedding altar by Marc Lambert?

31. What is the name of Sophie's child: Tamara, Tabitha, Tahnee or Tina?

32. Did Eric Pollard marry Gloria, Viv, Jackie or Katie in May 2002?

33. Which of these is a local *Emmerdale* newspaper: Hotten Courier, Emmerdale Messenger or the Weatherdale Express?

34. Who was the minister at St Stephen's Church?

35. Maria has a fling with John at the start of 2003, but who was John seeing at the time: Tracy, Toyah or Sally?

36. What is the name of the baby born to Emma Watts?

37. Which *EastEnders* character lived in the United States for most of her life?

38. Which launderette employee has lived for decades at number 45 Albert Square?

39. Colleen Smart is Alf's ex-wife: true or false?

40. Which male youngster had to have an operation after an accident at the boatshed: Dylan, Nick, Noah or Jade?

41. Who became a marketing executive for Ian Beale in Spring 2003?

42. Seb and Kirsty's Youth Week project was the trapping of their teacher: true or false?

43. Whose imprisonment was a major factor in Curly and Emma Watts' marriage problems?

44. Who swallowed a ring placed romantically in her wine glass by Bob Hope?

45. At the end of 2002, Mandy was having a liaison with: Max, Miles, Matt or Tony?

46. Who was Sally Fletcher's long-term boyfriend before she started to date Flynn?

47. Which *Emmerdale* lady did Bob Hope employ as a cleaner in May 2003?

48. Who arrived in 2003 claiming to be Colleen's daughter: Kylie, Annie, Maureen or Caitlin?

49. What is the name of Zoe Tate's daughter born in 2003?

50. Whose father tries to stop Phil Mitchell's September 2003 wedding?

 QUIZ 5

1. Who caught Louise's wedding bouquet: Steph, Ollie, Diane or Zoe?

2. Who throws a stone through Gail's window after losing her life savings to Richard Hillman?

3. Who was the long-standing doctor in the early years of *EastEnders*: Dr Foot 'n' Mouth, Dr Legg or Dr Andrews?

4. Does Boris Webster work as a car mechanic, an electrician, a butcher or a policeman?

5. Which daughter of Peggy's worked in Spain as a model and lapdancer?

6. Does Tracy Barlow, Boris Weaver, Maz O'Laughlin or Karen McDonald start working on the allotment?

7. Which member of the Ferreira family is a massive fan of Elvis?

8. Which family have lived at Wishing Well Cottage for a number of years?

9. Which older *Coronation Street* character was learning to drive in June 2003?

10. Chloe Bruce kidnaps OB after he played a practical joke on her: true or false?

11. Who does Roy sack after learning that they plan to open a rival café to his next door?

12. Who is Terry Woods' best man in his 2003 wedding?

13. Can you name either of the previous names of Lou's Place?

14. Jack Scully talks about moving back to his girlfriend Lori's home country. What is the country?

15. Who set fire to the Slaters' house and died in the process?

16. Who was the principal of Summer Bay High until he moved to be with his partner, June?

17. What is Felicity Scully usually called by the residents of Erinsborough?

18. What is the name of the brewery which has supplied the Rovers Return with beer for decades?

19. Edna Birch won a 2003 dancing competition with: Jack, Cain, Jarvis or Seth?

20. Seb, and which member of the Sutherland family, entered a photo competition in 2003?

21. Who won UNI FM's 'undiscovered' competition?

22. What was the name of the *Neighbours* family which included: Jim, Paul, Scott and Lucy?

23. Miles Mackie, Toby Mills or Tony Hutchinson posed as a film producer in *Hollyoaks*?

24. Who won the snogathon competition held at the Loft: Mandy and Adam, Zara and OB or Ellie and Ben?

25. Who was the youngest of the Scully family before the new baby arrived?

26. Who is stopped by OB from professing his feelings to his step-sister?

27. Which member of the Smith family lives in the Beach House with Irene?

28. Which *Neighbours* character is a builder and father of five children?

29. What is the name of the club which is a meeting place for local youngsters and was also the site of a Bonza Burger outlet?

30. Which *Hollyoaks* character was a professional footballer before moving into the leisure business?

31. What was the name of the bagpipes player from Tony's Burns Night event, who started dating Nick?

32. Albert Square's Fitness Centre was previously: a community centre, a video shop or the site of the original Queen Vic?

33. What is the name of Tariq Larousi's best friend's sister who he secretly dated?

34. Terry Woods was a former star in which sport: rugby, soccer, cricket or boxing?

35. Who tries to get Laurel sacked as the cleaner at the pub: Cain Dingle, Viv Windsor or Nicola Blackstock?

36. Which *Coronation Street* character wins a greenhouse while his wife thinks they've won a dream house?

37. Who became the owner of Evans & Sons car dealers after Roy Evans' death?

 38. Who attacked Donald Fisher and Morag, believing his dead wife told him to do so?

 39. Who offered Kit a bed for the night only to find their wallet stolen in the morning?

 40. What role does Dawn land in the Bollywood movie: an exotic dancer, a spy, a milkmaid or a female soldier?

 41. Who planned a TV cooking show only for it to fall apart when his two fiancées rowed?

 42. Which older *Emmerdale* resident beats Danny and other teenagers at a computer wrestling game?

 43. How did club owner Steve Owen die in *EastEnders*?

 44. Which son of Evan Hancock injured Harold and Leo when taking part in an illegal drag race?

45. Who challenged Tony to spend a day in a wheelchair?

46. Who gets knocked down by a car the day that Robbie and Nita are set to fly out of London?

47. What is the name of the shop next to the Queen Vic which employed Nita Mistry?

48. Martin and Katy trained for the London Marathon, the Weatherfield Fun Run or the Weatherfield Charity Football tournament?

49. Did Seb and Kirsty's photo come first, second or third in the photo competition?

50. What is the name of the band featuring Lee, Bombhead, Norman and Cameron?

QUIZ 6

1. Who was the owner of E20 who married Mel?

2. Which *EastEnder* was the mother of Simon and David Wicks?

3. Who lives at number 22 Ramsay Street: Harold, Lou or Karl and Susan?

4. Which one of the following celebrities has not appeared in *Coronation Street*: Joanna Lumley, Prince Charles, Will Young?

5. What special present did Steph buy her daughter, Tricia, on the eve of Tricia's wedding?

6. Which *Neighbours* character is a great singer but is nervous of singing in public: Steph Scully, Nina Tucker or Izzy Hoyland?

7. Who jilted Luke McAllister at the altar and ran away to go to University instead?

8. Name one of Gail's two previous husbands before Richard Hillman.

9. Who fell through the banisters of his own dodgy flats to die in 2002?

10. Fred Elliot accuses Harry, Karen or Shelley of stealing the money raised in memory of Maxine Peacock?

11. Tough guy Jack Dalton owns which club: Angie's Den, the Imperial Rooms, Zenon 52 or the Walford Golf Club?

12. Which two *Neighbours* sisters fell out over the affections of Marc Lambert?

13. Who got Anthony Trueman suspended from his job as a doctor?

14. Which *Coronation Street* lady was murdered in January 2003?

15. Which member of the Sutherland family had dreams of being a professional dancer?

16. Craig Dean is given a DVD player, a motorbike or a new suit by his mother who thinks he has done well in his exams?

17. Which scheming factory owner was formerly Mayor in *Emmerdale*?

18. Who offered to buy Rhys out of the caravan park to solve Rhys' money problems?

19. How many husbands has *Emmerdale's* postmistress, Viv, outlived: one, two, four or five?

20. Who tried to kill his mother-in-law in a house fire?

21. Mr C has a romantic fling with Izzy to get back at his wife's affair with Tony: true or false?

22. Who did Pauline plan a surprise 18th birthday party for at Angie's Den?

23. Who was the subject of Hayley's sculpture but had to be hospitalised when the plaster over his chest caused him to have breathing difficulties?

24. Who delivered an ant farm only to discover that the ants had escaped: Paul Marsden, Chris Tate or Seth Armstrong?

25. What is the name of the transport café in *EastEnders*?

26. Who does Lisa plan a game of badminton with in order to regain a ring taken by Lee?

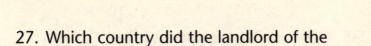

27. Which country did the landlord of the Woolpack for 43 years retire to?

28. What is the name of the Corrie supermarket which provided employment for Curly Watts and others?

29. Was Alex Healey, Alfred Legg or Alistair Cotton the vicar in *EastEnders* immediately before the arrival of Tom Stuart?

30. Who becomes extremely upset at news that Scott Hunter has a wife: Dani Sutherland, Sally Fletcher, Jade Sutherland or Hayley Smith?

31. How many wives has Ian Beale had in the show?

32. What is the nickname given to the house where Josh, Hayley and Noah have all lived?

33. Who spent their 18th birthday watching Jim and Dot get drunk?

34. Who works as a mechanic and fled his wedding when he learned his bride was having an affair with his best friend?

35. Summer Bay busybody Colleen Smart loves to fish to relax: true or false?

 36. Who tries to win his old partner back with the idea of a trip abroad?

 37. How did Tricia and Marlon leave *Emmerdale* straight after the wedding?

 38. Who pretended to have a panic attack in the swimming pool so that Izzy would jump in and rescue him?

 39. Which father had to endure the loss of two sons, Butch and Ben?

 40. What is the name of Joe Scully's father who he hadn't seen for many years?

 41. Which *Hollyoaks* mum is a mobile hairdresser by day and a club singer in the evening?

 42. What was the name of the group of school kids, determined to spread gossip, which was formed in *Hollyoaks*?

43. Joe Scully, Darcy Tyler or Connor O'Neil built up large gambling debts in 2003?

44. Who is the caretaker of Hollyoaks Community College: Matt, OB, Adam Morgan or Toby?

45. Did Stephen, Jade, Angie or Rhys tamper with Dylan's medical equipment while he lay in hospital?

46. What was the name of the newspaper editor who offered Libby a job but withdrew the offer when he learned that she was pregnant: Martin West, David East, Paul North or Jerry East?

47. Darren Turner was which *Neighbours* resident's ex-husband?

48. Which member of the Slater family took a break in Lanzarote after losing her baby?

49. Who, along with Max, was responsible for the Christmas Charity Grotto scam?

50. Which returning character creates a surprise by catching Kate Mitchell's bridal bouquet?

1. What was the name of the reality show set up in *Hollyoaks*: Big Bother, The Fish Tank or When Schoolkids Turn Bad?

2. Ian Beale lied to Mel that he had not long to live in order to get her to marry him: true or false?

3. Which member of the Sutherland family was a counsellor at the Drop-in Centre?

4. Alfie ordered male strippers, female strippers or a heavy rock band for the Vic, provoking outrage?

5. What was the cause of the foul smell at Lisa Dingle's house: Shadrach's trainers, a dead rat or Lisa's unwashed laundry?

6. Which one of the following has been the landlord of the Rovers Return: Curly Watts, Alec Gilroy or Les Battersby?

7. Who does Nick O'Conner share accommodation with: Jodie, Abby, Mandy or Izzy?

8. Who organised a saucy Men of Erinsborough fundraising calendar?

9. In the very first episode of *EastEnders*,
   Reg Cox was found dead in his house:
   true or false?

10. How does Richard Hillman first try to kill
    his family: by car fumes, with drugs or by
    driving in to a canal?

11. What is the name of Libby's first child?

12. Did Joe Scully, Karl Kennedy or Lori Lee
    deliver a baby during a bush fire?

13. Was Ian Beale's second wife: Mel, Cindy
    or Laura?

14. What is the name of the taxi firm in
    Coronation Street?

15. Who had a steamy weekend in Brighton
    with Jamie Mitchell when he was going
    out with Sonia?

16. Who went with Alf to the undertakers
    so that Alf could discuss coffins and
    grave plots?

17. Who reported Scott Hunter for not having
    a permit for the boathouse: Alf, Rhys, Josh
    or Lance?

18. Summer Bay High's school hall was named after who: Alf Stewart, Irene Roberts or Donald Fisher?

19. Libby received a journalism award for uncovering fixes in a game show called the Brain Game, Mind Over Matter, Brainbusters or Mind Games?

20. Which *EastEnder* won Minty's car in a card game: Jim, Dennis, Phil or Dot?

21. Which father is shocked to see his young daughter engaged in 2003?

22. Whose bracelet did Bombhead retrieve from the Police incident room?

23. Who viciously beat up Karen McDonald when their money-making scam went wrong?

24. Who stopped the hitman called George from killing Kate?

25. Who discovered that her fiancé, Carlos, was having an affair with her half-sister, Bernice?

26. Number 16 Coronation Street is: a garage, a newsagent, a café or a pub?

27. Who punched Tony over the Cunninghams' dinner table: Max, Mr C or Mandy?

28. Where did Libby go into early labour with her baby: at a rodeo, a country fair or a birthday party?

29. Who is the first friend of Ellie's to spot her dressed up as a giant spanner?

30. What nationality is Vinnie Patterson's widow?

31. What tube station serves the *Eastender's* Community: Walford East, Square Central, Walford Park or Walford West?

32. In the charity football match between the Woolpack and the Marsden family, who scored the winning goal?

33. Who wrote the play, Mission: Erinsborough, which received dreadful reviews?

34. Which *Neighbours* character is put on a kidney dialysis machine in 2003?

35. Who booked security man, George, for a job at the snooker hall using the fake name, Michael Batty?

36. Did Nick O'Conner, OB, Bombhead or Mandy Richardson help re-style Mr C to give him a younger look as he turned 50?

37. Who was Chris Tate's stepmother: Kim, Viv or Dawn?

38. Who knocked Syd Woolfe off his ladder with her car, putting Syd into hospital?

39. Donald Fisher helped which young vandal turn themselves into an award-winning artist?

40. OB and Max planned to record a song called 'Get Down With That Thing' with which surprising character on vocals?

41. Who gatecrashed Underworld's Christmas Party only to be forced to model lady's underwear?

42. Which two older *Neighbours* residents have both fancied Rosie Hoyland?

43. Vic Windsor died in a raid on the Post Office: true or false?

44. Who won £2,000 off Phil Mitchell in a poker game in April 2003?

45. Which *Coronation Street* star has had more than 20 different girlfriends in the show?

46. Which member of the Slaters married the day that Jamie Mitchell died?

47. Which member of *Hollyoaks'* The Fish Tank was paid extra by Chloe to flirt?

48. Who came to Summer Bay with Pippa and Tom and is now a teacher and counsellor?

49. Which two women fought over Neil's affections during New Year 2002?

50. What is the new name of the Octagon as revealed by Max?

1. Who bought back the Queen Vic pub in 2002: Peggy Mitchell, Pat Evans or Alfie Moon?

2. Which member of the Sutherland family was beaten up and robbed in March 2003?

3. Which woman did Zoe have an affair with only to learn that her brother had proposed marriage to her?

4. How long was Les Battersby's prison sentence for assault in 2003: 30 days, three months, six months or one year?

5. Name one of Kareena Ferreira's brothers.

6. Donald Fisher's files on Angie, Sally or Noah were destroyed in a deliberate fire at Summer Bay High in 2003?

7. Name one of Donald Fisher's two grandchildren.

8. Who resigned as Summer Bay's head lifeguard after failing to help a swimmer with a heart machine?

9. Lori Lee and Jack Scully lived together in which foreign city: London, Paris, Auckland or New York?

10. Did Karl Kennedy have an affair with his guitar teacher, his squash partner or his receptionist?

11. Which police officer covers for Hopwood's attack on Les Battersby?

12. Who had to go to hospital after a freak accident with a Christmas pudding: Jack Duckworth, Norris Cole, Vera Duckworth or Vik Desai?

13. What is the name of Tommy Nelson's wife?

14. Was the first death ever portrayed in *Emmerdale* in 1973, 1983, 1993 or 1999?

15. Who is the manager of the Loft club: Ellie Hunter, Chloe Bruce or Abby Davies?

16. Jack Sugden and Diane Blackstock organised the murder of Jack's wife, Sarah: true or false?

17. Who entered the Naughty Nylons Lovely Legs' competition which results in Bob Hope being sacked?

18. Who drove the car in the accident that left Adam paralysed?

19. Barry gets the locks changed in his house to prevent who from living there?

20. What is the name of Max Hoyland's sister who made her first appearance in 2003?

21. What household item did Maureen Slater hit Trevor with causing a court case?

22. Which *Coronation Street* youngster got her belly button pierced and ran off to take an audition to be in a pop band?

23. Which *Neighbours* character joins an over-35s football team and is found guilty of drunk driving in 2003?

24. Whose parents were *EastEnders* characters, Michelle Fowler and Den Watts?

25. OB, Max, Nick or Craig started to date a girl called Roxy over the Internet?

26. Who organised Tad and Paul's 18th birthday party?

27. Sarah finds which young *Coronation Street* character living in Sally Webster's old hardware shop: Ade Critchley, Candice Stowe, David Platt or Toyah Battersby?

28. Whose granddaughter is called Sky?

29. Where did the Kennedy's hide their valuable jewellery: in the fridge, under their bed, in their car glove compartment or behind the video recorder?

30. Who was Edna Birch's dancing partner before he sprained his ankle?

31. Who left his daughter in *Emmerdale* in January 2003 to move to a new job in Newcastle?

32. What was the name of Chris Tate's first wife?

33. What new reality show became a talking point in Summer Bay in 2003?

34. Who works at the bookmakers and had a black and white cat called Boots?

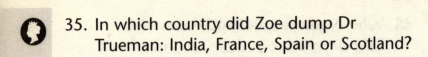
35. In which country did Zoe dump Dr Trueman: India, France, Spain or Scotland?

36. Did Pete, Jack, Tony or Luke pretend to be the new owner of the Loft at the start of 2003?

37. Which young *Neighbours* resident is Irish and on his arrival moved in with the Scully's?

38. Which member of the Dean family starts working as a lorry driver with Les Hunter?

39. Was Alex Poulos, Josh West or Jesse McGregor the Summer Bay lifeguard?

40. Which father used to keep whippets and has worked as a gardener at Home Farm?

41. Which biology student and son of two lawyers took Lisa Hunter to a rock festival?

42. Which *EastEnders* character has a doctor as his half brother?

43. What job did Laura Dunn work as for Ian before they got married?

44. Andy Sugden's real father was Billy Hopwood, Jack Sugden or Bob Hope?

45. Who was appointed bar manager of the Rovers Return in July 2002?

46. Who confessed to killing Angie Russell only for it to be found he was lying?

47. Who sends a picture of a bare bottom on Max's new video mobile phone?

48. Whose ex-husband is to be released in 2003 from prison?

49. Who suffered minor burns along with Jim when the vat of illegal alcohol exploded?

50. Which character was released from Strangeways prison in the late summer of 2003?

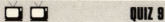 **QUIZ 9**

1. Which niece of Jack Osborne made her first appearance in *Hollyoaks* in late May 2003?

2. Is Phil's car mechanics business housed in the Arches, on Turpin Road or next to the allotments?

3. Sarah has a 16th birthday party at her house when her Mum, Gail, is away in: Spain, France, Canada or Portugal?

4. Which girl was suspended from school for bullying Andy Sugden?

5. Lou and Lolly ran away to a caravan park: true or false?

6. Who taught Martin Fowler to drive: Derek Harkinson, Phil Mitchell or Robbie Jackson?

7. Ellie, and which man, were left in charge of the pub when Jack Osborne had to travel to London?

8. Who broke-in to the Kennedy's house knocking Lyn Scully unconscious as a result?

9. Who is Alfie Moon's little brother: Spencer, Mark, Martin or Jack?

10. Who sold photographs of Debbie and Dan in the back of Tony's car to a local newspaper?

11. Which Woolfe arrived in *Emmerdale* to work on Viv Hope's café building?

12. Which Corrie ladies have an argument which ends with both of them falling into a swimming pool?

13. Where did Dee Bliss work?

14. What landmark *Coronation Street* building was burned down in 1986?

15. Who formerly ran a driving school before moving into property and a discount shop?

16. How many weddings did *Coronation Street* see in 1999?

17. Who is the widow of *Coronation Street's* long-serving mayor, Alf?

18. Which *EastEnders* character has had four husbands?

19. Which teenager was born in a taxi and saw her parents, Sally and Kevin divorce?

20. Who did Billy convince to dress up as an alien at an event night at E20?

21. What name was Kath's Café changed to when it came under new ownership?

22. What is Dot Cotton's surname now that she is married to Jim?

23. Angie Reynolds worked as a Japanese translator, a poet, a postlady or a policewoman?

24. Which one of the following characters featured in the very first episodes of *EastEnders*: Jim Branning, Peggy Mitchell, Sharon Watts or Zoe Slater?

25. Who organises for Sindi Watts to see Toadfish in order to keep Toadfish and Dee Bliss apart?

26. Whose underwear is framed as a piece of art: OB's, Kristian's, Max's or Mr C's?

27. Policeman Will Davies has two children. Can you name his daughter?

28. Who was found guilty of killing a school head teacher: Marc Reynolds, Butch Dingle, Paddy Kirk or Bob Hope?

29. Who is the owner of the Dog in the Pond?

30. What was the name of Shadrach's brother who was the father of Tina Dingle?

31. Who was best man at Curly and Emma's wedding: Steve McDonald, Ashley Peacock or Martin Platt?

32. Which mother of a large Summer Bay family ran away at the end of 2002?

33. Which *Neighbours* character left Erinsborough to play football with the Adelaide Crows?

34. Who did Sally ask to be her matron of honour at her wedding to Flynn?

35. What was the first name of Alf's wife of many years?

36. What is the name of Max Hoyland's son?

37. What is Marlon Dingle's middle name: Elvis, Sebastian, Zak or Cain?

38. Laurel Potts' night at Marlon and Tricia's engagement party ended with: a burst appendix, a broken arm or a bump on the head?

39. Louise Carpenter, Lou's stepdaughter, was better known as Lou-Lou, Lolly or Isa?

40. Which boy has one sister and a policeman for a father?

41. Irene and Sally set up a trap for which school busybody?

42. Does Darcy break into a Ramsay Street house to steal money, jewellery, a priceless vase or a stamp collection?

43. Whose great-grandfather was one of the first settlers in Summer Bay: Alf, Irene, Rhys or Colleen?

44. Who ran the bait shop in Summer Bay?

45. Whose parents returned to *Neighbours* in 2003: Toadfish's, Max's or Connor's?

46. Can you name the two Beale twins?

47. Who left their old home and moved into Jacob's Fold in February 2003?

48. Who had a cleaning business in *Emmerdale* before Laurel Potts: Nicola Blackstock, Bernice Thomas or Dawn Hope?

49. Was Nick found guilty or innocent of the attack on Angie Russell?

50. Who is Lee disappointed to see getting friendly with Abby in September 2003: Craig, OB or Bombhead?

QUIZ 10

1. Who married a much younger bride in 2003?

2. Flick travels with which *Neighbours* character on a disastrous camping trip in January 2003?

3. What is the full name of the *Emmerdale* character known as Mack?

4. What was Angie's Den previously called?

5. Zara was less than impressed when her new car turned out to be previously owned by: Scott Anderson, Tony Hutchinson or Mr Cunningham?

6. Who is Kat's grandmother?

7. Who proposed to Maria Sutherland at the top of Blackpool Tower?

8. Who took over the ownership of Kath's Café when Ian Beale was made bankrupt?

9. Spider Nugent was an environmental campaigner whose Aunt was Emily Bishop, Annie Walker, Vera Duckworth or Betty Williams?

10. Which couple got remarried in December 2002?

11. Which new arrival at the Drop-in Centre turns out to be Scott Hunter's sister?

12. Which *EastEnders* character has Mark and Martin Fowler as uncles?

13. Who set up two hidden cameras to catch Angie admitting how she had tried to ruin Nick Smith's life?

14. Which *Neighbours* character wrote and staged a musical in 2003?

15. Irene took Trevor, Paris or Alf to the fundraising dance in April 2003?

16. Who robbed MOCO and nearly let Steph Scully go to jail for it?

17. Which notorious *Hollyoaks* landlord once fitted a waste processing septic tank with disastrous results?

18. Who cut her trip with Alex short to come back to Erinsborough to declare her love for a different man?

19. Louise Appleton shocked the village when she started going out with which elderly character?

20. How old was Sarah Platt when she had her baby: 13, 15 or 16?

21. Bob Hope decided to stay in *Emmerdale* after talking to his daughter, his wife or his grandmother?

22. James Willmott-Brown ran the Dagmar, the Queen Vic or E20?

23. Where did Andy and Katie go to live after leaving Ollie's house?

24. Is Carl Bromley, Jack Walker or Grant Bailey the owner of a large rival car dealers to Barry's business?

25. What degree subject did Sally take at University: Archaeology, English, History or Geography?

26. Which character became pregnant by Darcy Tyler who then left her on her own?

27. What is the name of the church in *Neighbours*: St Robert's, St Thea's or St Stephen's?

28. Who sold the Loft to Scott Anderson but kept a 10 percent share?

29. What was the name of Charlotte Adam's lost boyfriend who visited her shortly before she died?

30. Lyn Scully's occupation is: a teacher, a minister, a vet or a hairdresser?

31. Who is the owner of the Gnosh restaurant in *Hollyoaks*?

32. Which interfering busybody is a parish councillor and first appeared in 2000?

33. Who was best man at Steve and Karen McDonald's wedding: Vik Desai, Ashley Peacock or Kevin Webster?

34. Who did Cindy Beale attempt to have killed with an armed hit man?

35. Who did Seb Miller live with after Donald Fisher left Summer Bay?

36. Whose son is an oil rig worker and owns a half share in Lou's Place?

37. Whose class was held at gunpoint by Woody: Sally, Donald or Angie?

38. Who had a miscarriage in 2002: Katie Addyman, Ollie Reynolds or Zoe Tate?

39. What is the 'heavenly' name of the underworld boss who is an enemy of Paul Trueman?

40. Which family held a 2002 fireworks night for *Hollyoaks* residents: the Morgans, the Cunninghams, the Deans or the Hunters?

41. Which one of the following is Ricky's sister: Janine, Natalie or Sam?

42. Who accidentally burned his adopted mother to death in a barn fire?

43. The *Hollyoaks* serial killer first struck in January 2002, July 2002, December 2002 or March 2003?

44. Which villainous character murdered Maxine and killed his ex-partner Tricia with a spade?

45. A scan on Sophie reveals that she is carrying one baby, twins or triplets?

46. What was Curly Watt's first job in *Coronation Street*: supermarket manager, bin man, barman or butcher?

47. Ex-*Hollyoaks* characters Finn and Lewis opened up which venue still present in the village?

48. Who was mugged by Stephen's friends in January 2003?

49. Who found Norman lying hurt in the gutter after being beaten up: Max, OB, Mr C or Jake Dean?

50. Which young girl won two weeks of free riding lessons in September 2003?

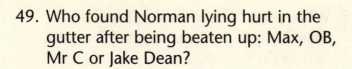
QUIZ 11

1. What is the name of the club, beginning with the letter A, which holds gambling evenings in Erinsborough?

2. What was Spider Nugent's real first name: Gerry, Geoffrey or George?

3. In 2000, *Coronation Street* celebrated its 20th, 30th, 40th or 50th birthday?

4. Who did Dr Anthony Trueman nearly marry before going out with Kat Slater?

5. Bob Hope worked at Naughty Nylons, Sexy Silks or Cheeky Cottons as a sales rep before becoming a manager for Eric Pollard?

6. Who spent the day in a wheelchair in May 2003 to try to understand what it was like?

7. Whose poor eyesight nearly caused a major truck crash: Joe, Tad or Karl?

8. Which new arrival in 2003 bought Alf's old boathouse?

9. Which father and son both try to court Dale Jackson?

10. Who tried to stop the robbers of the Minute Mart only to be arrested for the robbery?

11. What is the name of Angie's daughter who has an affair with Angie's ex-lover?

12. Who had to sell her old wedding dress to finance her second attempt at marrying the same man?

13. Martin Fowler's father's first name was Tony, Frank, Roy or Arthur?

14. Who gave Ben a black eye in April 2003: Bombhead, Izzy, Scott or Jodie?

15. Whose fiancée died of a drug overdose in jail: Jesse, Vinnie or Noah?

16. What do Seb, Kirsty, Jade and Nick discover near the Sutherland's house: a cave, a suitcase full of cash or a nest of rare bird's eggs?

17. Which Slater sister hasn't lived in the square and is married to Neville?

18. Who married Butch Dingle on his deathbed?

19. Which couple dressed as a bride and groom for a bridal fair held at Lassiters?

20. Who is the step-sister of Jude and Cindy?

21. Marlon Dingle won £500, £5,000, £15,000 or £50,000 on a lottery scratch card game?

22. Which *Neighbours* family did Toadfish live with after his own family moved out of Ramsay Street?

23. Who finds Angie dead in her home when he visits to hand her back things from the gym?

24. Nina, and which other character, are given a detention for fighting at school?

25. Where did Andy and Katie move into when it was discovered that Katie was pregnant?

26. Dennis Rickman's father was Pete Beale, Den Watts, Frank Butcher or Roy Evans?

27. Who was Seth Armstrong's childhood sweetheart who returned to live with him?

28. Which joker in *Emmerdale* found the tables turned when he took temporary charge of the Woolpack pub?

29. Who did Connor split up with just after the Immigration department almost make him leave Australia?

30. Homeless Norman was offered a place to stay at the Cunninghams, in the Loft or in the Dog in the Pond pub?

31. Which young *Coronation Street* girl left the show in Spider's van travelling down to London?

32. Which couple married in Knowsley Hall, a posh country house, in July 2002?

33. Guy, Lauren and Ling Mai were all children of Lou Carpenter's: true or false?

34. Which *EastEnders* hard man gave Sonia a laptop computer for her 18th birthday?

35. Sunita, and which other *Coronation Street* woman, rowed over Ciaran in early 2003?

36. Who was demoted as factory supervisor when Joe became a partner with Mike Baldwin?

37. Irene's boyfriend, Ken, was also the father of Hayley, Noah or Josh?

38. Who started training girls to play soccer: Noah, Alex, Nick or Rhys?

39. Who pretended Sutton Grange was his home: Mike Baldwin, Wally Bannister, Richard Hillman or Les Battersby?

40. Who runs Erinsborough's pub?

41. Who is Nathan Williams' half-brother?

42. Who appeared at Tricia and Marlon's engagement party dressed as a bumble bee?

43. Toby lived in Ibiza before coming to work for Jack in the Dog in the Pond pub: true or false?

44. What was the name of the young female doctor who died in a beach accident?

45. After Alf returned from his near death experience he started organising candlelit dinners at the diner: true or false?

46. Who put a £20,000 offer in for Steve McDonald's house in January 2003: Wally Bannister, Peter Barlow, Richard Hillman or Jack Duckworth?

47. What was the first name of Dr Trueman's mother?

48. Which pop hero of Tony's does he meet at a student graduation party: Kylie Minogue, Darius, Mel C or Emma Bunton?

49. What is the first name of Dr Anthony Trueman's real father: Patrick, Peter or Paul?

50. Who bought a plot of land from Rodney in the belief it contained ancient gold?

 **QUIZ 12**

1. Who threatens to throw Ellie out of the house if she continues her plans to hold a pole dancing evening?

2. Who got Dani fired as a journalist from a local newspaper?

3. Tony Hutchinson got engaged to two women at the same time: one was Julie, who was the other?

4. Which member of the Slater family hosted a saucy underwear party in July 2003?

5. Who saved Lolly from drowning in the swimming pool: Max Hoyland, Darcy Tyler or Boyd Hoyland?

6. Where did Katie Addyman move to after rows with her fiancé, Andy, about how he treated Stephen?

7. Whose first journalistic assignment is investigating Max and Colleen's fake book?

 8. Which new boarder in the Sutherlands house cut up many of Dani's clothes in a fit of anger?

 9. What is Flynn's surname?

 10. Who was the ant farm to be delivered to: Ollie, Victoria or Viv?

 11. Who rekindles a romance in 2003 with the new Principal of Summer Bay High?

 12. What is the name of the dog in the Kennedy's household: Alfie, Audrey, Amber or Alfa?

 13. Which female college student dated Max in the past and has been College President?

14. Which young girl steals the affections of an old wealthy man from her grandmother?

15. Which elderly Corrie resident spent a night up a tree with her eco-warrior nephew to save the 'red rec'?

16. Who did Pauline organise a leaving party for at the launderette in March 2003?

17. Who is upset at the loss of her Aunt Nina's ring: Debbie Dean, Mandy Richardson, Sally Morgan or Helen Cunningham?

18. Nicola Blackstock first appeared in 2001 as whose long lost sister?

19. Who helps Bob Hope out at the Post Office and has a crush on him?

20. Who does Jack Scully blame for Lori's swimming pool accident?

21. Who gave birth in Tony's shop: Anna, Helen or Cindy?

22. Tyrone Dobbs' dog was called Fido, Monica, Mitchell or Mutley?

23. Which real life DJ and ex-pop star made a *Hollyoaks* appearance as himself in the New Year's Eve 2002 episode?

24. What is the name of Cain and Charity's daughter?

25. Who was engaged to Fred Elliot at the start of 2003: Blanche, Audrey or Doreen?

26. Which *Neighbours* family included Emily, Evan and Leo?

27. Who married Paddy Kirk in October 2002?

28. Which couple had their hen and buck's parties on the night of Ben's 1st birthday?

29. Who raided a safe rather than help Duggie Ferguson as he died: Mike Baldwin, Dev Alahan or Richard Hillman?

30. Who tries to assist Carl Bromley in his takeover of Barry's car business?

31. What was the name of Dot's errant son?

32. What was the name of Curly Watts' first wife?

33. What was the subject of the advert which used Seb and Kirsty's competition photo: haircare products, petrol, lipstick or bad breath?

34. How many children do Frankie and Johnno Dean have?

35. Rosie Hoyland kissed which character whilst being unaware that the church was on fire?

36. After recording Angie's mistreatment of Nick, where does Seb set up his video cameras next: the nursing home, the bait shop or Summer Bay High?

37. What is the name of Bernice Thomas's daughter?

38. Did Asif Malik, Arthur Fowler or Jim Branning once steal and trash Steve Owen's car?

39. Was news of the second *Hollyoaks* murder broadcast on Christmas Eve, New Year's Eve or Easter Sunday?

40. Which member of *Emmerdale* is famous for his deerstalker hat and moustache?

41. In which country did Deirdre meet her boyfriend, Samir Rachid?

42. Who arranges for Mack to gain an unfair advantage in obtaining the job to repair the village hall roof: Edna, Diane, Steph or Chris?

43. Jesse McGregor has a daughter he had to leave when he went on the run. What was her name?

44. Which son of Dirty Den Watts arrived in the Square in 2003 after spending three years in prison?

45. What is the name of Ian Beale's fish 'n' chip shop?

46. Who is the youngest brother of the Ferreira family?

47. Harold Bishop had a daughter who married legendary *Neighbours* character: Dr Clive Gibbon, Des Clarke, Joe Mangel or Paul Robinson?

48. Which *EastEnders* youngster bought a consignment of chart CDs only to discover they were in the charts four decades ago?

49. Cain Dingle has slept with a mother and a daughter from which family?

50. Who is remanded in prison after being falsely accused of stealing money from the minicab office?

 QUIZ 13

1. Who jumped onto the dance podium in the Loft, performed a half striptease but fell and twisted his ankle?

2. After the Bayside Diner burned down, what was the name given to the new diner opened by Alf and Ailsa?

3. Wally Bannister owns a mansion: true or false?

4. Which two *Hollyoaks* lads found themselves both sharing a date with Roxy?

5. What degree subject did Adam Morgan study at Hollyoaks Community College?

6. Who receives divorce papers from his wife on Valentine's Day 2003?

7. What is the name of the hairdressers at Lassiters: Short and Curlies, A Good Hair Day, Hair Today – Gone Tomorrow or Clippers?

8. Which elderly member of the *EastEnders* cast was sent to prison for 14 days?

9. Which daughter of Kerry Bishop and Eric Jensen returned to Ramsay Street as a nightmare teenager in 2003?

10. Who offered Phil Mitchell £5000 to act as a hitman in 2003?

11. Did Barry and Natalie celebrate their wedding anniversary on New Year's Eve, Christmas Day or Easter Monday?

12. Who did Robbie go to India with in 2003?

13. Who does Lori catch naked in the kitchen at night when she is staying at the Kennedy's house?

14. What was the name of Little Mo's first husband who frequently hit her?

15. Which girl has a sister called Debbie and a brother called Craig?

16. Who moved into Tricia and Marlon's house while they were away in India?

17. What is the name of Kat Slater's father?

18. Which member of the aristocracy left *Emmerdale* with Sean Reynolds?

19. Which family ran the Rovers Return in the past for 40 years: the Ogdens, the Lynchs the Walkers or the Duckworths?

20. Which young member of *Coronation Street* was diagnosed as a diabetic in 2003: Rosie, Katy, Sarah or Fiz?

21. Who was left with purple hair when Audrey left Maria and Candice Stowe in charge of her hair salon?

22. Who married Toby Mills in July 2003?

23. Whose parents were killed in a boating accident when she was just three: Leah, Sally, Irene or Hayley?

24. Nana is: Alfie, Martin, Asif or Paul's grandmother?

25. Who was the first landlord of the Woolpack: Seth Armstrong, Amos Brearly or Viv Windsor?

26. Who succeeds Donald Fisher as the new permanent head of Summer Bay High: Sally, Angie or Paris?

27. Who sent a picture of Harold Bishop modelling a curly afro hairstyle on email?

28. What is the name of Dylan Russell's mother?

29. How many contestants does the *Hollyoaks* reality TV show have: three, five, seven or nine?

30. Is Roy's Rolls found on George Street, Victoria Street, Grasmere Terrace or Coronation Street?

31. What is the name of Hayley's friend who has a crush on Alex: Caitlin, Amber, Kit or Constance?

32. Which *EastEnders* character works as a lecturer and has an MA in English Literature?

33. What is the name of Lisa's daughter by Phil Mitchell?

34. What was the name of Hilda Ogden's husband?

35. Who arrived in *Emmerdale* to become the village postmistress: Cynthia Daggert, Betty Eagleton or Viv Windsor?

36. One of the Dingle clan's first name is Charlton: true or false?

37. Which *Neighbours* mother has Valda Sheergold as her aunt?

38. Stuart Parker was struck down by malaria, hypothermia or scarlet fever on a January 2003 camping trip?

39. What is the name of Charity's husband?

40. Who hit Josh, after Josh had started to move in on his girlfriend?

41. Who received a mixed reception in 2003 when they announced that they were getting married?

42. Harold turned the coffee shop into what modern facility?

43. Which of the following is not a neighbouring town of Summer Bay: Yabbie Creek, Murrayville or Mangrove River?

44. Which student in Summer Bay suffers from epilepsy?

45. Which brother and sister killed Liam and hid all the evidence?

46. Who took Brodie out on a boat in order to propose to her but didn't have the nerve?

47. Who turned out to be Zoe's mother: Kat, Laura or Pat?

48. Who hit Ray Mullan with a vase on Boxing Day 2002?

49. Chloe Atkinson and Scott Windsor split up after Chloe slept with which character?

50. What is the name of the baby born to Lucy Richards and Peter Barlow?

1. Who inherited Mill Cottage after Ray Mullan's death?

2. Who on New Year's Eve 2002 confesses to having feelings for Phil Mitchell?

3. Which number Ramsay Street becomes a boys-only zone known as the House of Trouser?

4. Was the local Corrie undertaker called Archie Shuttleworth, Norris Cole or Fred Elliot?

5. Who turned up dressed as a giant banana at Mark Fowler's stag do?

6. Who had a one-night stand with Beth and also a relationship with Steph?

7. Who did Natalie have an affair with in 2003?

8. In March 2003, a new lodger moved into the Cunninghams' house who was having an affair with one of the family. Who was the new lodger?

9. Maggie Smart is the mother, daughter, sister or cousin of Lance Smart?

10. What is the first name of the lady who ran the newsagents in *Coronation Street* for many, many years?

11. Who slipped on some milk, hit her head and forgot the past 30 years of her life?

12. Which father and son team ran the used car lot in the Square: Roy and Barry, Arthur and Mark or Alan and Robbie?

13. What does Ellie end up dressed as in her first sales promotion job?

14. Who is Hayley Smith's younger brother?

15. What is the name of the school featured in *Neighbours*: Ramsay Primary, Erinsborough High, St Andrews Secondary School or St Stephen's High?

16. When Curly split up from Emma in May 2003, where did he spend the night?

17. What is the name of Irene Roberts' son who spent time in jail: Neil, Nathan, Greg or Paul?

18. What was the name of Martin Fowler's elder sister?

19. Phil Weston arrived in *Emmerdale* when he crashed into Maggie Calder's car: true or false?

20. Which building contractor and club owner won the heart of Louise Blackstock for a while?

21. Where did Ailsa Stewart die: in the flat above the diner, outside the bait shop, on the beach or in New Zealand?

22. Did Phil Mitchell, Peggy Mitchell or Grant Mitchell present Jamie with a socket set on his 18th birthday?

23. Alex fought with his brother at his 21st birthday party. What was Alex's brother's name?

24. Which member of the Dingle clan shares a first name with a very famous rock 'n' roller?

25. Who threw water on a chip fat fire which caused the Bayside Diner to burn down: Alf Stewart, Colleen Smart or Ailsa Stewart?

26. Which family live at number 28 Ramsay Street?

27. Who became Landlord of the Rovers Return in May 2002?

28. Who killed Carol's dog and tried to replace it: Lewis, Finn or Tony?

29. Who was arrested for the *Hollyoaks* murders only to admit that he was having an affair with Steph Dean?

30. Who worked as a chef for Eric Pollard and married Tricia in 2003?

31. Will Smith has a younger sister. What is her name?

32. Who failed to get a teaching job at Erinsborough High and took a post in the country instead?

33. Who attempted suicide when he was only given 24 hours to pay his debts to Chris Tate?

34. Which son of a wealthy businessman had a long relationship with Dani Sutherland?

35. What is the first name of the lapdancer who set Scott Windsor up in August 2003?

36. Which teenager has a brother called Mobashir?

37. Who is Les Battersby's estranged wife?

38. Which girl shared a flat with Nick and had to put up with his boyfriend, Nathan?

39. Who rescued Gail Hillman from the car in the canal?

40. Which two men ended up having a brawl over the affections of Ellie?

41. What is the name of Nita's son?

42. Who offered Charity £5000 to move out of her house?

43. What is the name of the lake in Erinsborough?

44. Which former bin man became a local councillor in *Coronation Street*?

45. AFL selector Giles Peterson offers which Ramsay Street resident a big chance to play AFL football?

46. Who did Robbie share the money from his real dad with: Sonia, Pauline, Asif or Gus?

47. How many children do Karl and Susan Kennedy have?

48. Taj Coppin was the captain of his school football team: true or false?

49. What is the name of *Emmerdale's* churchman and father of Gabrielle?

50. Who is asked to be best man at Phil Mitchell's wedding to Kate and arranges Phil's stag night?

QUIZ 15

1. When Raquel left Curly did she first move to: Malaysia, Australia, Canada or London?

2. Phil Weston had one daughter who accompanied him to *Emmerdale*. What was her name?

3. Who organised a surprise wedding for herself to take place on Valentine's Day, 2003?

4. How many dollars did Darcy tell Dee he had lost gambling: $1,000, $10,000, $100,000 or a million dollars?

5. Which former owner of the Rovers Return worked in redeveloping flats with Richard Hillman until his death?

6. What was the name of Sharon's pet poodle: Roly, Truffles or Fido?

7. What is the name of the launderette business in *Hollyoaks* owned by Mrs Cunningham?

8. Which lady leaves Erinsborough to go to a mission in Papua New Guinea?

9. Which of Rosie's grandchildren is in an accelerated learning program for bright children?

10. What is the name, beginning with the letter V, of the lady who steps in when Lou's cook quits?

11. Which *Hollyoaks* character had a brother called Theo who died?

12. Who along with Chloe planned the reality TV show which occurred in *Hollyoaks*?

13. What is the name of Paul Trueman's daughter: Elizabeth, Eleanor or Edith?

14. In what year did Mr C marry Helen: 1998, 1999, 2000 or 2001?

15. After working in journalism, what occupation did Libby Kennedy study for?

16. Who did Sam have a fling with the night before her birthday in 2003?

17. What is the name of Lance Smart's mother?

18. Who was attacked from behind during the night that an earthquake struck *Hollyoaks*?

19. What was the name of Robbie Jackson's dog?

20. The Coffee Shop has been known by three other names. Can you recount one of them?

21. Whose antiques barn did Danny Daggert work in for a short while: Rodney Blackstock, Jack Sugden or Eric Pollard?

22. Which student is forced to study at Yabbie Creek High after his court case?

23. Who was suspended from their teaching job for punching Aidan Critchley on the nose?

24. What is the name of the daughter Curly had with Raquel?

25. Did Ricky Butcher elope to Spain, Up-West or to Gretna Green to marry Sam Mitchell?

26. Who became a bride in March 2003: Dawn Hope, Kelly Windsor or Bernice Thomas?

27. Who boycotts the corner shop after Dev Alahan has plans to build an amusement arcade near their business?

28. Who was arrested by the police for illegally selling raffle tickets and holding stolen goods?

29. Which businessmen was married to Dee de la Cruz until she left him?

30. DI Dove frequently questioned Louise Blackstock over the death of which man?

31. Which two ladies have worked in the launderette for many years?

32. Who gave Darcy another chance at the surgery: Flick, Karl or Susan?

33. Which member of the Dingle family has been engaged to Paddy Kirk and has worked in the Post Office?

34. Where did Shelley Unwin work before the Rovers Return: Underworld, the Kabin or the rugby club?

35. Where did Irene Roberts work before her job at Summer Bay High?

36. Who is Andy Sugden's adopted father?

37. What is the name of Ollie Reynolds' brother: Zak, Marc, Luke or Paul?

38. Which former husband and wife compete against each other for catering business?

39. Jack Duckworth won a year's supply of dog food, toilet cleaner, washing powder or lager in May 2003?

40. Who was attacked by a fake charity collector and found unconscious on the floor by Jim?

41. Who lost her brother, Jamie, and changed her hair colour from blonde to black?

42. Who is the first girl in Summer Bay to take an interest in Scott Hunter?

43. Who opened the Vic for Martin Fowler's coming back to Walford party?

44. Pauline Fowler was pregnant with Martin in the very first year *EastEnders* started: true or false?

45. Max Sutherland's father is: Pete, Rhys, Vinnie or Tom?

46. Who has an ex-wife called Alison, a son called Ben and had an affair with Sue Morgan?

47. Who started to peddle DVD players in 2003?

48. Alex gave Leah a cheque to help buy a house. Was the cheque for $5,000, $25,000, $50,000 or $100,000?

49. Who ruins his A-Level exam paper and walks out of the exam hall whilst his ex-girlfriend watches on?

50. Which gangland businessman takes over Jack Dalton's empire?

QUIZ 16

1. Which *Hollyoaks* character is a diabetic and refused to give a DNA sample to the police making him a suspect in the murder investigation?

2. Who was blinded at the end of the historical tribute to Alf Stewart and his family?

3. Where was Alex's 21st birthday party held?

4. Which young girl has dated Jamie, Paul Trueman and Billy?

5. Who was Tracy Barlow dating before getting interested in Wally Bannister?

6. Which is the youngest of the Webster children: Rosie or Sophie?

7. Who was concerned about Norman and offered him a job collecting glasses?

8. Who made Becca Hayton pregnant: Jamie, Bombhead, Alex or OB?

9. Which *Emmerdale* character has a grandfather called Len and studied for her exams in 2003?

10. Who stole Boyd's clothes in revenge for Boyd spying on her?

11. Which lady, already a mother of a number of children, became pregnant in 2003?

12. Who rushed Les Battersby to hospital only to crash his car and die?

13. Which former member of the 80s pop group, Spandau Ballet, played a memorable villain in *EastEnders*?

14. Who built the new Roy's Rolls café in Victoria Street: Kevin Webster, Steve McDonald or Les Battersby?

 15. Who attacked Roxy with a spanner?

 16. Which Summer Bay newcomer started dating Alf Stewart and has a love of fishing just like Alf?

 17. Who became Viv Windsor's third husband?

 18. Which member of the Dingles was upset when Stella the tortoise was accidentally packed with an order and posted?

 19. Who did Spencer Moon snog on New Year's Eve 2002: Kelly, Janine, Laura or Zoe?

 20. Who inherited an allotment from one of his old friends: Jake Dean, Abby Davies, Ben Davies or Craig Dean?

 21. Who gave up drinking after losing his driving licence in 2003?

 22. Which of the following characters took part in a speed dating competition at Lou's Place: Max, Toadfish, Harold or Boyd?

23. Who organises a collection to buy Dot a new crucifix: Jim, Phil, Peggy or Pauline?

24. Who is the older brother of Noah Lawson?

25. Who was Dirty Den's wife throughout the early days of *EastEnders*?

26. Who overstays his welcome at Paddy and Emily's house and asks to move back in with Lisa?

27. Who is asked to do the catering for what turns out to be his own wedding party?

28. Whose father was killed by a marksman at Home Farm?

29. Did Lyn, Harold or Steph convince Jack to become coach of the girls soccer team?

30. Who tries to smother Steph whilst she lays in hospital: Bombhead, Toby or Abby?

31. What is the name of Harold Bishop's lodger who bought him a nude female sculpture as a present?

32. Chloe Lambert and which other character were tied up and robbed in 2002?

33. What is the name of Scott's wife who visited Summer Bay in 2003: Mary, Mira, Michelle or Mandy?

34. Who danced with Abby Morgan to win the ballroom dancing competition: Lee Hunter, Jake Dean or Tony Hutchinson?

35. Who rents Todd a shambles of a flat above the bookmakers?

36. Who leaves Ben and OB naked after a game of strip poker: Izzy, Steph or Chloe?

37. Which *Home and Away* character declared his love for Sally just days before her wedding to Flynn?

38. In their market stall wars with the Slaters, which family gives away free CDs in order to increase their sales?

39. How much money is Karen to pay Mike Baldwin so he doesn't call the police: £800, £8,000 or £80,000?

40. Jack told Lori that he had been having an affair with Nina, Tahnee or Lyn?

41. Who asks Hayley to be unpaid supervisor at the clothing factory after sacking Karen?

42. What is the name of Vinnie Patterson's father: Ray, Ronnie or Ralph?

43. Who struggled to make a decision about going to film school in New York in June 2003?

44. Who sent a video apologising that he cannot attend Sally's wedding only to suddenly appear as a surprise?

45. Who did Lyn ask at Lassiters to be godmother to her unborn child?

46. Whose van catches fire after being looked after by Lee and Bombhead?

47. Whose joy at completing his first driving lesson was tempered by fears that his café was infested with insects?

48. Who collapsed and went into labour at Sally's hen party?

49. Which female *Neighbours* character returned in 2003 after being kicked out of a New York exchange programme?

50. Laurel entered a competition using other people's names but who actually walked off with the Cruise prize?

HARD
Questions

1. Who murdered former Queen Vic Landlord, Eddie Royle?

2. What revision device does Danny muck around with causing a row with its owner, Ollie?

3. Who beat up Vik Desai for making them part of a drugs smuggling operation from Tenerife to Weatherfield?

4. Which of Bob Hope's stepchildren flirted with him when he first arrived in *Emmerdale*?

5. What was the 'valuable' name of Paul Trueman's ex-girlfriend?

6. What sort of antique, worth over £200,000, did Steph plan to dupe Rodney Blackstock out of in the spring of 2003?

7. Who came across photographs of the women murdered by the serial killer and suffered nightmares as a result?

8. Emma Jackson was the character played by which Australian pop star?

9. Who was first arrested on suspicion of the murder of Maxine Peacock?

10. Belinda Peacock seduced one young *EastEnders* character when she was having a crisis in her marriage. Who was it?

11. What was the name of the village before it was called Emmerdale?

12. Who was Mike Baldwin married to before Linda?

13. Zara persuaded which *Hollyoaks* character to pretend to be a famous pop star in order to help with the sale of the Morgans' house?

14. What is the name of the lady Donald Fisher leaves Summer Bay to join in Queensland?

15. What was the name of Kylie Minogue's character in *Neighbours*?

16. Who does OB try to convince Max he should start dating in May 2003?

17. Who does Candice have a fight with over the affections of Jason Grimshaw at Sarah's 16th birthday party?

18. What is the first name of Bob Hope's ex-wife?

19. Who kidnapped Mel Owen and issued a ransom for £200,000?

20. With whom did Linda Sykes have an affair shortly before marrying Mike Baldwin?

21. How many children did Helen Cunningham have from her first marriage?

22. What newsagents was redeveloped as the local Post Office in 2000?

23. Steph had an affair with Brian when he was going out with which *Hollyoaks* teenager?

24. Who jumped out of a cake at Des's buck's party in the very first episode of *Neighbours* only to go on and marry Des?

25. Who were the first owners of the Queen Vic pub in *EastEnders*?

26. Whose Munch Box mobile burger van was closed by a public health inspector?

27. Who enters their place of work to find their daughter in a coma in intensive care?

28. Who bared all to Mrs Cunningham in what used to be the Steam Team premises?

29. Who fell down the stairs in 2003 with the suspicion being that Alf pushed her?

30. Who told Steph that Mitch had set fire to a factory and killed someone?

31. Which *Home and Away* original cast member lost her first husband to a heart attack while her second husband drowned?

32. Which grandmother was an artist in Ramsay Street and owner of Home James chauffeurs?

33. How many grade 'A' passes does Martin announce that Asif got in his June 2003 exams?

34. Who jilted Tony Hutchinson at the altar?

35. What was the name of the Japanese girl which was Sam's first love?

36. Which female character was Summer Bay's resident lifeguard before leaving?

37. Which student first appeared in Ramsay Street as the girlfriend of Jack Scully?

38. Who came to Summer Bay to see her kids, Finn and Damien, who were in foster care?

39. Who was the last member of the di Marco family to leave *EastEnders*?

40. Who was a chef at Hollyoaks College before being sacked?

41. Who was injured in the Barlow's car when it was stolen and driven by Ade Critchley?

42. Steph Scully takes a romantic interest in a barman in 2003 but what is his name?

43. Which partner of Sophie's arrived in Summer Bay after hearing Sophie was pregnant?

44. Who told Mr C the truth about his wife's affair with Tony Hutchinson?

45. What is the name of the choir organised by Rosie Hoyland?

46. Which Summer Bay resident inherited two million dollars and was to fund orphanages with the money?

47. What number Albert Square do the Slater family live at?

48. Who tipped salad over Steph in the Woolpack in spring 2003?

49. Which Doctor harasses Dee: Dr Darcy, Dr Cook or Dr Kennedy?

50. Lee's first attempt at going solo from the boy band, X-Factor, is sabotaged by which other *Hollyoaks* character?

1. Who did Spencer buy a massive consignment of baked bean tins from?

2. To whom did Richard Hillman first admit that he had killed Maxine Peacock?

3. What was the first name of the limo driver with whom Viv had an affair on Tricia's hen night?

4. Who is in goal for the Woolpack football team when the penalty is scored past him in April 2003?

5. Who was the only experienced cave potholer on the trip which saw two *Hollyoaks* characters die?

6. Which family live at 26 Ramsay Street?

7. What was the name of Helen Cunningham's son who died in *Hollyoaks*?

8. Who stepped in to be best man at Mike Baldwin's wedding to Linda?

9. Who was Ricky first married to?

10. In what year did a plane crash devastate the village and kill a number of villagers?

11. What number *Coronation Street* is the Post Office located at?

12. How many road workers help carry Tony Hutchinson up a set of stairs in his wheelchair only to chase him when he stands up?

13. Police Constable Hopwood was living with whose partner when the pair fought?

14. Luke Morgan briefly returned from which country for a family wedding?

15. Who suffered a terrible motorcycle accident along with Libby Kennedy?

16. Scott was played by which singing star in *Neighbours*?

17. Who, apart from Chloe and Matt, moved in to Mandy's old flat at the start of 2003?

18. Peter Barlow had a twin sister who died in a car crash. What was her name?

19. How much money did Rodney pay for the mill in a September 2003 property auction?

20. Which detective from Newcastle became friendly with Phil Mitchell?

21. Who took Maria Sutherland to Barbados when he was running away from his gambling debts?

22. Name one of the two characters who died in a potholing crash in November 2002.

23. Who gave birth to a son called Byron in Summer Bay?

24. Who mistakes Taj Coppin as her secret admirer?

25. Gus got the job as the market sweeper after who resigned?

26. Who became the face of the Holiday Village only to quit the job to work in the Café Hope?

27. Who got remarried in a Manchester prison in 2000?

28. Which friend of Lisa's turns out to have a major interest in ice hockey?

29. Who told Kirsty that Seb Miller gave her a mystery kiss in the dark?

30. After Valda's makeover of Lou's Place, what are the waiters dressed up as?

31. What was the first name of Irene's boyfriend who was crushed to death when a car slipped off its jacks?

32. Who drove the car which killed Tiffany in 1998?

33. Which *Hollyoaks* male went out with his college lecturer, Christine, for a while?

34. Which member of the Dingles made their first appearance at Butch's funeral where she stole Eric Pollard's wallet?

35. Which Summer Bay male rescued Charlotte Adams from drowning only for her to die in hospital later?

36. Which *EastEnders* character has both a brother and a son called Jack?

37. Who converted the Scully's garage into his bedroom?

38. A successful book which the whole of Summer Bay thought was written by Colleen turns out to be written by which other character?

39. What is the name of the Indian Restaurant in *EastEnders*?

40. What is OB's full name?

41. Libby Kennedy's magazine was first called 'Demo' but what was it called afterwards?

42. What is the name of Alf Stewart's son?

43. Who moved into Mr C's house in April 2003 and surprisingly did the cooking and cleaning?

44. Who poisoned Michelle because he couldn't read labels?

45. Who is qualified as a doctor and came to Summer Bay in his search for his missing sister?

46. Which Vicar married Dot and Jim?

47. Who stuffed a glove down the toilet to flood the Woolpack pub?

48. Who refereed the Walford World Cup football competition?

49. Rhona Goskirk was a temporary vet who had an affair with which member of the Dingle family?

50. Which long-serving barmaid and landlady left *Coronation Street* in the mid-1990s but returned for a brief period in 2002?

EASY
Answers

1. The Dingles
2. Walford
3. Lou's Place
4. The Slaters
5. Wheelie bins
6. FALSE
7. Adam Morgan
8. A garden allotment
9. Darius
10. Flynn

11. Helen Cunningham
12. Richard Hillman
13. Manchester
14. Jack Sugden
15. The Sutherlands
16. TRUE
17. Pauline
18. Susan Kennedy
19. Alf
20. TRUE

21. FALSE
22. Natalie
23. Jesse
24. Phil
25. Paul
26. Colleen Smart

27. Cain Dingle
28. Steve
29. A policewoman
30. Duckworth

31. Scott
32. The Rovers Return
33. The Fowlers and the Beales
34. Ramsay Street
35. Scott
36. London
37. Pat
38. Toby Mills
39. Hilda Ogden
40. The Dog in the Pond

41. A Bollywood film
42. Summer Hoyland
43. TRUE
44. In Spain
45. Alf Stewart
46. Lassiters
47. Arthur
48. Harold Bishop
49. TRUE
50. Izzy

1. Summer Bay
2. Natalie Imbruglia
3. The Queen Vic

4. Yorkshire
5. Kangaroo
6. A cure for baldness

7. Mike Baldwin
8. Tony Hutchinson
9. Dingle
10. FALSE

11. Hayley Smith
12. Erinsborough
13. Female
14. A poacher
15. Underworld
16. Hollyoaks Community College
17. A florists
18. A bonsai tree
19. 31 years
20. Madge

21. Bonza Burger
22. Walford
23. Red
24. TRUE
25. Dan Hunter
26. Summer Bay High
27. Dr Karl Kennedy

28. Sonia
29. The Woolpack
30. Deirdre and Tracy

31. TRUE
32. Norman
33. Debbie Dean
34. Sally Fletcher
35. Edna Birch
36. TRUE
37. Craig
38. TRUE
39. Fiz
40. Theo

41. Marlon
42. Mandy Richardson
43. Audrey's
44. A pub lunch
45. Scottish
46. Deirdre
47. His car
48. Rosie
49. Gypsy
50. USA

QUIZ 3

1. Toadfish
2. Line dancing
3. Todd and Jason
4. Chester
5. Joshua
6. Toilet paper
7. Jack Sugden
8. Vicki Fowler
9. Harold Bishop
10. Jade Sutherland

11. Jack
12. Dawn Hope
13. Max

14. Kit Hunter
15. £10,000
16. Donna
17. TRUE
18. Norris Cole
19. Donna
20. The Truemans

21. Dione
22. Danni Minogue
23. Anthony Trueman
24. Dr Karl Kennedy
25. Peter
26. Roy Cropper

27. The College (Hollyoaks Community College)
28. Roy's Rolls
29. The Woolpack
30. FALSE

31. Dylan
32. Chooka
33. Barry Evans
34. A builder
35. VJ
36. Emma Watts
37. Pole dancing

38. Eve
39. Laura
40. Boyd Hoyland

41. FALSE
42. TRUE
43. Weatherfield
44. £1,000
45. Peter Barlow
46. Matt
47. Underwear
48. Taj
49. Pushpa
50. Eddie Hope

MEDIUM Answers

QUIZ 1

1. Toadfish
2. Ronnie Marsden
3. Paddy Kirk
4. Ben
5. Jesse McGregor
6. Scott Anderson
7. Tony Hutchinson
8. Mal
9. A riding accident
10. Dev Alahan

11. Chloe Atkinson
12. Pushed off a cliff
13. Sally Webster
14. 2001

15. Ben
16. Barry
17. TRUE
18. TRUE
19. Debbie
20. Kelly

21. FALSE
22. Billy Mitchell
23. Peter Barlow
24. Karl Kennedy
25. Jodie
26. Colleen
27. The Chronicle
28. The Queen Vic

29. A heart attack
30. Gavin

31. Harold Bishop
32. Jarvis
33. Maria
34. Lori
35. TRUE
36. Mandy Richardson
37. Gnosh Village
38. Dani Sutherland
39. Hayley Cropper

40. Trevor Morgan

41. Eric Pollard
42. Dev Alahan
43. A mudslide
44. Alfie Moon
45. Shelley Unwin
46. TRUE
47. Bob Hope
48. Scott Windsor
49. Dan Hunter
50. Harold Bishop

QUIZ 2

1. Male stripper
2. Norman
3. Vinnie
4. Dev Alahan
5. Clare
6. Bob
7. Lee
8. Zara
9. Joe
10. Chloe Bruce

11. Dr Trueman
12. Maggie Hancock
13. A gambling addiction
14. Jim Branning
15. E20
16. A butcher
17. Charity
18. Alex Poulos
19. Ken Barlow
20. Law

21. Irene Roberts
22. A video tape
23. 1999
24. Syd Woolfe
25. Sean Reynolds

26. Heather
27. Janice Battersby
28. The Davies' house
29. Leah
30. Johnno

31. Ireland
32. Angie Russell
33. Roy and Hayley Cropper
34. Debbie
35. Max Hoyland
36. Hayley
37. Zoe Tate
38. FALSE
39. Alison
40. Alfie Moon

41. Kristian
42. Kirsty Sutherland
43. Mike Baldwin
44. Ken Barlow
45. Danny Daggert
46. Kelly Taylor
47. Ricky Butcher
48. Craig Dean
49. Suzie
50. Terry Windsor

QUIZ 3

1. Charity Tate
2. Stephanie Scully
3. Kate
4. £25,000
5. TRUE
6. Shadrach
7. Ollie
8. India
9. Roy Cropper
10. Toby

11. Leah Poulos
12. Martin Platt
13. Wilf
14. TRUE
15. Australian Rules Football
16. Daniel's Dad
17. Sarah Platt
18. Chris Tate
19. Ailsa Stewart
20. Jason Grimshaw

21. FALSE
22. Izzy Cornwall
23. Barry Evans
24. Watches
25. Alfie Moon

26. Max
27. Summer Hoyland
28. Gordon Cunningham
29. Her jacket
30. Chris Tate

31. Gus
32. Angie Russell
33. Tracy Barlow
34. Cheryl
35. Sophie
36. Tricia
37. Drew Kirk
38. Tad Reeves
39. Lucy Benson
40. Andy Sugden

41. Bethany
42. Craig Dean
43. Tommy Nelson
44. FALSE
45. Jack Dalton
46. Donald Fisher
47. OB
48. Ricky
49. Tahnee Coppin
50. Jack and Vera Duckworth

QUIZ 4

1. Richard Hillman
2. Big Kev
3. Linda
4. Sarah Beaumont
5. Ben Davies
6. Maxine Peacock
7. Kristian
8. Harry Slater
9. Craig Dean

10. Barnsford

11. Number 32
12. Tricia
13. Work as a teacher
14. An earthquake
15. Jade and Kirsty
16. Eric Pollard
17. Pat

18. A heart attack
19. Scott
20. Martin Fowler

21. Crimea Street and Victoria Street
22. Dot
23. Phil Mitchell
24. TRUE
25. Mr C
26. Joanne Ryan
27. Duggie Ferguson
28. Marlon
29. Jack Scully
30. Stephanie

31. Tamara
32. Gloria
33. Hotten Courier

34. Rosie Hoyland
35. Toyah
36. Ben
37. Vicki Fowler
38. Pauline Fowler
39. FALSE
40. Dylan

41. Sam Mitchell
42. TRUE
43. Les Battersby's
44. Viv
45. Miles
46. Vinnie Patterson
47. Laurel Potts
48. Maureen
49. Jean
50. Kate Morton

QUIZ 5

1. Diane
2. Vera Duckworth
3. Dr Legg
4. A butcher
5. Sam Mitchell
6. Maz O'Laughlin
7. Dan Ferreira
8. The Dingles
9. Roy Cropper
10. FALSE

11. Ciaran
12. Chris Tate
13. Chez Chez or The Waterhole
14. New Zealand
15. Trevor Morgan
16. Donald Fisher
17. Flick
18. Newton and Ridley

19. Jarvis
20. Kirsty

21. Nina Tucker
22. The Robinsons
23. Miles Mackie
24. Ellie and Ben
25. Michelle
26. Max
27. Nick Smith
28. Joe Scully
29. The Surf Club
30. Scott Anderson

31. Nathan
32. A community centre
33. Kareena Ferreira
34. Rugby
35. Nicola Blackstock
36. Jack Duckworth

37. Barry
38. Alf Stewart
39. Noah
40. A milkmaid

41. Tony Hutchinson
42. Len Reynolds
43. The car he was in exploded

44. Matt Hancock
45. Adam
46. Wellard (Robbie's dog)
47. The Minute Mart
48. The Weatherfield Fun Run
49. It came first
50. X-Factor

QUIZ 6

1. Steve Owen
2. Pat Evans
3. Lou
4. Will Young
5. Tricia's old wedding dress
6. Nina Tucker
7. Tina Dingle
8. Brian Tilsley and Martin Platt
9. Duggie Ferguson
10. Harry

11. The Imperial Rooms
12. Steph and Felicity (Flick) Scully
13. Kat Slater
14. Maxine Peacock
15. Jade Sutherland
16. A DVD player
17. Eric Pollard
18. Josh West
19. Two
20. Richard Hillman

21. FALSE
22. Martin Fowler
23. Alex
24. Paul Marsden

25. Laura's Cafe
26. Abby
27. Spain
28. Freshco
29. Alex Healey
30. Dani Sutherland

31. Three
32. The Palace
33. Sonia
34. Stuart Parker
35. TRUE
36. Ronnie
37. In a hot air balloon
38. Ben Davies
39. Zak Dingle
40. Pat Scully

41. Frankie Dean
42. The Rumour Club
43. Darcy Tyler
44. Matt
45. Stephen
46. Martin West
47. Dee Bliss
48. Kat Slater
49. OB
50. Lisa

QUIZ 7

1. The Fish Tank
2. FALSE
3. Shelly Sutherland
4. Male strippers
5. Shadrach's trainers
6. Alec Gilroy
7. Jodie Nash
8. Rosie Hoyland
9. TRUE
10. By car fumes

11. Ben
12. Joe Scully
13. Mel
14. Streetcars
15. Zoe Slater
16. Donald Fisher
17. Josh
18. Donald Fisher
19. Brainbusters
20. Dennis

21. Bob Hope
22. Steph's
23. Joe Carter
24. Phil Mitchell
25. Nicola Blackstock
26. A garage

27. Max
28. At a rodeo
29. Toby
30. Greek

31. Walford East
32. Ali Marsden
33. Harold Bishop
34. Lou Carpenter
35. Phil Mitchell
36. Nick O'Conner
37. Kim
38. Emily
39. Hayley Smith
40. Mr C

41. Les Battersby
42. Lou Carpenter and Harold Bishop
43. TRUE
44. Ian Beale
45. Ken Barlow
46. Little Mo
47. Ellie Hunter
48. Sally Fletcher
49. Steph and Nicola
50. Gnot Gnosh

QUIZ 8

1. Peggy Mitchell
2. Rhys
3. Charity
4. Six months
5. Ronny, Adi, Ash
6. Angie
7. Seb Miller and Sam Marshall

8. Josh West
9. London
10. His receptionist

11. Emma Watts
12. Norris Cole
13. Angela
14. 1973

15. Ellie Hunter
16. FALSE
17. Viv Windsor
18. Mandy
19. Pat
20. Izzy Hoyland

21. An iron
22. Rosie Webster
23. Karl Kennedy
24. Vicki Fowler
25. OB
26. Flick
27. Ade Critchley
28. Harold Bishop's
29. In the fridge
30. Len Reynolds

31. Brian Addyman
32. Kathy

33. The Dorm
34. Shirley Benson
35. Scotland
36. Pete
37. Connor O'Neil
38. Johnno Dean
39. Josh West
40. Brian Addyman

41. Kristian
42. Paul Trueman
43. A nanny
44. Billy Hopwood
45. Shelley Unwin
46. Rhys Sutherland
47. OB
48. Helen Cunningham's
49. Patrick
50. Les Battersby

QUIZ 9

1. Natalie Osborne
2. In the Arches
3. Canada
4. Donna Windsor
5. TRUE
6. Derek Harkinson
7. Toby
8. Darcy Tyler
9. Spencer
10. Steph

11. Syd Woolfe
12. Deirdre and Tracy
13. Erinsborough Hospital
14. The Rovers Return
15. Mr C (Gordon Cunningham)
16. Four
17. Audrey Roberts

18. Pat Evans
19. Rosie Webster
20. Janine

21. Laura's
22. Branning
23. A policewoman
24. Sharon Watts
25. Darcy
26. Kristian's
27. Abby Davies
28. Marc Reynolds
29. Jack Osborne
30. Zak

31. Ashley Peacock
32. Shelley Sutherland
33. Paul McClain
34. Leah

35. Ailsa
36. Boyd Hoyland
37. Sebastian
38. A burst appendix
39. Lolly
40. Ben Davies

41. Angie Russell
42. Jewellery

43. Alf
44. Alf Stewart
45. Toadfish's
46. Lucy and Peter
47. Ollie and Len
48. Nicola Blackstock
49. Guilty
50. Craig

QUIZ 10

1. Terry Woods
2. Stuart Parker
3. Jerry Mackinley
4. E20
5. Tony Hutchinson
6. Mo
7. Tyrone Dobbs
8. Phil Mitchell
9. Emily Bishop
10. Kevin and Sally Webster

11. Kit
12. Vicki Fowler
13. Seb Miller
14. Harold Bishop
15. Trevor
16. Mitch
17. Tony
18. Steph Scully
19. Rodney Blackstock
20. 13

21. His daughter
22. The Dagmar
23. Butler's Farm
24. Carl Bromley
25. Archaeology

26. Dee Bliss
27. St Stephen's
28. Tony Hutchinson
29. Jude Lawson
30. A hairdresser

31. Tony Hutchinson
32. Edna Birch
33. Vik Desai
34. Ian Beale
35. Alf Stewart
36. Rosie Hoyland
37. Sally
38. Katie Addyman
39. Angel
40. The Deans

41. Janine
42. Andy Sugden
43. July 2002
44. Richard Hillman
45. Twins
46. Bin man
47. The Loft night club
48. Katie Addyman
49. OB
50. Summer

QUIZ 11

1. The Aurora Club
2. Geoffrey
3. 40th birthday
4. Zoe Slater
5. Naughty Nylons
6. Tony Hutchinson
7. Joe
8. Scott Hunter
9. Ben and Will Davies
10. Gus

11. Ollie
12. Tricia
13. Arthur
14. Izzy
15. Jesse
16. A cave
17. Belinda
18. Emily
19. Toadfish and Dee
20. Mandy Richardson

21. £15,000
22. The Kennedys
23. Jesse
24. Taj
25. The Woolpack

26. Den Watts
27. Betty Eagleton
28. Bob Hope
29. Michelle
30. The Dog in the Pond pub

31. Toyah Battersby
32. Gail and Richard Hillman
33. TRUE
34. Phil Mitchell
35. Shelley
36. Hayley Cropper
37. Hayley
38. Alex
39. Wally Bannister
40. Lou Carpenter

41. Barry Evans
42. Laurel Potts
43. TRUE
44. Dr Charlotte Adams
45. TRUE
46. Peter Barlow
47. Audrey
48. Darius
49. Patrick
50. Eric Pollard

QUIZ 12

1. Sally
2. Angie Russell
3. Izzy Cornwall
4. Little Mo
5. Darcy Tyler
6. Ollie Reynold's house.
7. Dani Sutherland
8. Kit Hunter
9. Saunders

10. Victoria

11. Irene Roberts
12. Audrey
13. Chloe Bruce
14. Tracy Barlow
15. Emily Bishop
16. Dot
17. Sally Morgan

18. Bernice Thomas
19. Mrs Rudge
20. Taj

21. Cindy
22. Monica
23. Boy George
24. Debbie
25. Doreen
26. The Hancocks
27. Emily Dingle
28. Karl and Susan
29. Richard Hillman
30. Janine

31. Nick
32. Raquel (Wolstenholme)
33. Bad breath

34. Four
35. Lou Carpenter
36. The nursing home
37. Gabrielle
38. Asif Malik
39. New Year's Eve
40. Seth Armstrong

41. Morocco
42. Edna
43. Rachel
44. Dennis Rickman
45. Beale's Plaice
46. Adi Ferreira
47. Joe Mangel
48. Spencer
49. The Reynolds
50. Eileen

QUIZ 13

1. OB
2. The Beachside Diner
3. FALSE
4. Kristian and OB
5. Media Studies
6. Les Battersby
7. A Good Hair Day
8. Dot
9. Sky Mangel
10. Jack Dalton

11. New Year's Eve
12. Nita
13. Karl Kennedy
14. Trevor
15. Steph Dean
16. Paul and Siobhan
17. Charlie Slater
18. Lady Tara Thornfield
19. The Walkers
20. Katy

21. Vera Duckworth
22. Ellie Hunter
23. Sally
24. Alfie
25. Amos Brearly
26. Paris
27. Tahnee Coppin
28. Angie
29. Five
30. Victoria Street

31. Amber
32. Ash Ferreira
33. Louise
34. Stan
35. Viv Windsor
36. TRUE
37. Lyn Scully
38. Hypothermia
39. Chris Tate
40. Noah

41. Toby and Ellie
42. An internet café
43. Murrayville
44. Nick
45. Chris and Zoe

46. Alex
47. Kat
48. Louise Blackstock
49. Syd Woolfe
50. Simon

QUIZ 14

1. Louise Blackstock
2. Joanne Ryan
3. Number 30
4. Archie Shuttleworth
5. Gary
6. Scott Anderson
7. Ricky
8. Tony Hutchinson
9. Daughter
10. Rita

11. Susan Kennedy
12. Roy and Barry
13. A giant spanner
14. Nick Smith
15. Erinsborough High
16. Jack and Vera's house
17. Nathan
18. Michelle
19. TRUE
20. Ray Mullan

21. In the flat above the diner
22. Phil Mitchell
23. Dimitri
24. Elvis Dingle
25. Colleen Smart

26. The Kennedys
27. Fred Elliot
28. Finn
29. Scott Anderson
30. Marlon Dingle

31. Hayley
32. Libby
33. Wilf
34. Josh West
35. Yolanda
36. Asif Malik
37. Janice
38. Jodie
39. Tommy Nelson
40. Scott and Toby

41. Anish
42. Zoe
43. Lassiter's Lake
44. Curly Watts
45. Paul McClain
46. Sonia
47. Three
48. TRUE
49. Ashley Thomas
50. Rick 'Minty' Peterson

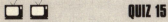 ## QUIZ 15

1. Malaysia
2. Jess
3. Tricia

4. $10,000
5. Duggie Ferguson
6. Roly

7. Washed Up
8. Rosie Hoyland
9. Boyd Hoyland
10. Valda

11. Norman
12. Adam Morgan
13. Eleanor
14. 1999
15. Teaching
16. Dennis Rickman
17. Colleen Smart
18. Ben Davies
19. Wellard
20. Daphne's, The Hungry Bite and the Holy Roll

21. Rodney Blackstock
22. Nick Smith
23. Ken Barlow
24. Alice
25. Gretna Green
26. Dawn Hope
27. Roy Cropper
28. Max Sutherland

29. Eric Pollard
30. Ray

31. Pauline and Dot
32. Karl
33. Emily Dingle
34. The rugby club
35. The Beachside Diner
36. Jack Sugden
37. Marc
38. Laura and Ian
39. Toilet cleaner
40. Dot

41. Jodie
42. Dani Sutherland
43. Alfie Moon
44. TRUE
45. Pete
46. Will Davies
47. Lou Carpenter
48. $50,000
49. Todd Grimshaw
50. Andy Hunter

 QUIZ 16

1. Dan Hunter
2. Alf
3. The Surf Club
4. Janine Butcher
5. Dev Alahan
6. Sophie
7. Jack Osborne
8. Jamie
9. Ollie Reynolds
10. Lori

11. Lyn Scully
12. Dennis Stringer
13. Martin Kemp

14. Steve McDonald
15. Toby Mills
16. Maureen
17. Bob Hope
18. Sam Dingle
19. Kelly
20. Jake Dean

21. Karl Kennedy
22. Max and Harold
23. Jim
24. Jude Lawson
25. Angie Watts
26. Marlon

27. Marlon Dingle
28. Scott Windsor
29. Lyn
30. Toby

31. Gino
32. Darcy Tyler
33. Mira
34. Lee Hunter
35. Peter Barlow
36. Izzy
37. Mikey
38. The Ferreiras

39. £8,000
40. Nina

41. Mike Baldwin
42. Ralph
43. Adam
44. Donald Fisher
45. Susan
46. Max's
47. Roy Cropper
48. Sophie
49. Tahnee
50. Viv Hope

HARD
Answers

QUIZ 1

1. Nick Cotton
2. A memory tape
3. Steve McDonald
4. Kelly
5. Precious
6. A mermaid figurine
7. Abby
8. Danni Minogue
9. Aidan Critchley
10. Jamie Mitchell

11. Beckindale
12. Alma Sedgewick
13. Lee
14. June Reynolds
15. Charleen

16. Jodie
17. Katy Nelson
18. Jean
19. Dan Sullivan
20. Mark Redman

21. Two
22. The Kabin
23. Zara
24. Daphne
25. Den and Angie Watts
26. Mandy Dingle
27. Martin Platt
28. Bombhead
29. Morag
30. Woody

31. Pippa
32. Helen Daniels
33. Three
34. Julie
35. Tomiko
36. Shauna Bradley
37. Lori Lee
38. Irene Roberts
39. Beppe
40. Max

41. Sarah Platt
42. Alex Argenzio
43. Blake
44. Max
45. The Erinsborough Angels
46. Dr Charlotte Adams
47. Number 23
48. Nicola
49. Dr Cook
50. Craig Dean

QUIZ 2

1. Mickey
2. Gail (his wife)
3. Matti
4. Bob Hope
5. Kristian
6. The Scullys
7. Lewis
8. Roy Cropper
9. Sam Mitchell
10. 1993

11. Ten
12. Three
13. Les Battersby's
14. Canada
15. Stephanie Scully
16. Jason Donovan
17. Becca
18. Susan
19. One million pounds
20. Kate Tyler

21. Vik Desai
22. Jamie and Theo
23. Marilyn
24. Nina Tucker
25. Ben

26. Chloe Atkinson
27. Jim and Liz McDonald
28. Cameron
29. Nick Smith
30. Samurai Warriors

31. Ken
32. Frank Butcher
33. Adam Morgan
34. Charity Dingle
35. Josh West
36. Natalie Evans
37. Connor O'Neil
38. Max Sutherland
39. The Argee Bhajee
40. Sam O'Brien

41. New Voice
42. Duncan
43. Bombhead
44. Connor
45. Flynn Saunders
46. Reverend Tom Stuart
47. Nicola Blackstock
48. Derek Harkinson
49. Marlon Dingle
50. Bet Lynch (Bet Gilroy)